THE CHURCH AND PASTOR'S GUIDE TO THE LAW

by Walker O'Duggan

Copyright 2012
Green Creek Publishing Company

CONTENTS

Chapter I.
Introduction
Chapter II.
What Is A Church?
Chapter III.
Constitutional Law
Chapter IV.
Statutory Law
Chapter V.
Unincorporated Church Societies
Chapter VI.
Incorporated Religious Societies
Chapter VII.
Superior Authority
Chapter VIII.
Inferior Authority
Chapter IX.
Membership
Chapter X.
Heresy And Secession
Chapter XI.
Excommunication
Chapter XII.
Elections
Chapter XIII.
Officers
Chapter XIV.
Meetings
Chapter XV.
Church Records
Chapter XVI.

Church Tribunals
Chapter XVII.
State Courts
Chapter XVIII.
Evidence
Chapter XIX.
Contracts
Chapter XX.
Pews
Chapter XXI.
Property
Chapter XXII.
Religious Services
Chapter XXIII.
Bequests, Devises, And Gifts
Chapter XXIV.
Taxation
Chapter XXV.
Eleemosynary Institutions
Chapter XXVI.
Schools
Chapter XXVII.
A. Counseling in Church, B.Parent And Child
Chapter XXVIII.
Husband And Wife
Chapter XXIX.
Indians
Chapter XXX.
Juvenile Courts
Chapter XXXI.
Libel And Slander
Chapter XXXII.
Crimes
Chapter XXXIII.
Cemeteries
Chapter XXXIV.
Funding International Operations
Chapter XXXV
Taxes and the Clergy
Chapter XXXVI

THE CHURCH AND PASTOR'S GUIDE TO THE LAW

The contents of this book was compiled through research with information coming from many sources. It is compiled with the feeling of completion, however something that you feel important may have been left out. For any errors or omissions I ask for your forgiveness. The law firm of Thompson and Thompson in Livona, MI, had a wealth of information on their web site and I recommend that before starting a church you contact them or another attorney who understands church law. Judging by the Thompson and Thompson web site I personally feel that they are well versed in what you will need.

One thing for certain is that the law will change. The law is like a river, always moving and changing direction. City, County, State and Federal Laws along with the IRS laws will change. This is a guide to be used to assist you. What you find in this guide will not replace an attorney or a CPA. This is only a tool that will enable you to a quicker understanding of the law as it pertains to the church and it's dealings. For tax or IRS questions consult a tax attorney or a CPA. Never, never make legal decisions without consulting an attorney first.

The three learned professions, medicine, law, and theology, overlap; and a man who does not know something of the other two can not be prominent in his own. Laws relating to Church matters are scattered through such a vast array of law books that it would be a burden for a clergyman to purchase them, and without special training he would not know where to look for the law. Therefore a law compendium covering those subjects relating to Church matters must be of great value to a clergyman.

There is another view of this subject. When civilization was young the laws of the Roman Empire were for the Roman citizens, particularly the patricians; the canon law was the law of the Christian people of conquered countries and the Christian plebeians of Rome. In the United States we have the same common law for the President and the log-splitter, for the multimillionaire and the penniless orphan, for the clergy and the laity. Consequently, in this practical age a knowledge of the law of the country with which the clergy come constantly in contact is expedient, if not necessary.

The poet says:
"What constitutes a state?... Men, who their duties know, But know their rights,

and knowing, dare maintain."

To insure harmony and good order, every Church should obey the laws of the country; but if any law should impose upon the rights of the Church in any way, the ruling authorities, the cardinal and bishops, if the wrong is national, should unite in a petition to the United States Congress, clearly stating the grievance and asking for its redress.(1) If the grievance should be within a State, the bishop or bishops of the State should present the matter to the Legislature of the State. If the President or the Governor has authority to remedy the matter, go direct to him. Such was the practice of the wisest of the Popes.(2) The author never knew of an instance in which a clergyman having a real grievance failed in obtaining a full and fair hearing from the powers that be, from the President downward. This method seems to be more in harmony with the relations of Church and State in a free government, and more intelligent than to have a convention of working men, who have little time to make a study of Church matters, pass resolutions, the passing of which generally ends the action of a convention.

In the chapters that follow, the author has refrained from giving a great multitude of authorities, but has endeavored to give such as are sufficient to sustain the text. For example, under the first section, and many others, a list of citations covering several pages might be given. That would add to the expense of the volume and would not be within its compass. The book will better fulfill its purpose by clear, brief statements of the rules of law, and if a reader desires to investigate further, the citations given will guide his way. The internet has a wealth of information.

CHAPTER I.
INTRODUCTION

1. *Law, Religion.*--From the dawn of the science of law it has been influenced by religion or antagonism to religion. This is very evident in the ancient laws of Babylonia, Egypt, Phoenicia, Israel, India, and Ireland. It would be impossible to make a study of the law of any of said countries without gaining a knowledge of its religious system, whether pagan or otherwise.(3)

2. *Religions.*--Ancient nations might be classified into pagan and those that worshiped the universal God. However, some of the nations at one time were pagan and at other times had a fair conception of the supernatural. Also, in Egypt, the class of higher culture and education believed in the one omnipotent and omniscient Being, but the populace, who could be controlled more readily by flattering them in their notions and giving their childish conceptions full sway, worshiped idols.(4)

3. *Authority, Right.*--In those nations where the ruling authority had the proper conception of the Almighty, there was a strong, persistent growth of law upon the basis of natural right; while in the pagan nations laws were arbitrary and despotic.(5)

4. *Philosophical Foundations.*--The laws of Greece, down to the time of Plato, were thoroughly pagan. But, following the philosophical foundations laid by Plato and Aristotle, unintentionally and unwittingly the laws of Greece became imbued with the spirit of natural law.(6)

5. *Rome, Natural Justice.*--Prior to the introduction of Grecian law into Rome, the laws of that nation were pagan. Grecian law from its introduction to the time of Octavius was the civilizing element of the empire. Then it took a turn for the worse, the element of natural justice being reduced and the element of arbitrary rule becoming dominant.(7)

6. *Canon Law.*--We will now turn to the first period of canon law, which covers the early history of the Church up to the reign of Constantine the Great.(8) Canon law is composed of the following elements:

1. Holy Scriptures; 2. Ecclesiastical tradition; 3. Decrees of Councils; 4. Bulls and rescripts of Popes; 5. The writings of the Fathers; 6. Civil law.(9)

7. *Early Christians.*--Owing to the persecutions, the early Christians were, in a sense, isolated from the State; they held their property in common, and were governed in matters among themselves by the canon law. However, for want of freedom of discussion and publication, they were unable, even within a single nation of the empire, to promulgate a system of canon law. The foundation of canon law being laid, its development upon the manumission of the Church was rapid.(10)

8. *Persecutions, Defenses.*--During the religious persecutions the Christians almost had law forced into them by surgical operations. The necessity for their making defenses in the Roman tribunals induced many of them to give Roman law a careful study. Also, the great number of Christians held for trial on all sorts of accusations made that branch of the law of the realm very lucrative for lawyers, and called into the field many Christians. Incidentally, men studying for the priesthood made a study of Roman law with a view to avoiding its machinations and continuing their functions as clergymen without being caught in the net of persecution.(11)

9. *Constantine, Blending the Law.*--When Emperor Constantine became a Christian (325 A.D.), there was a great change, and the members of the bar and judges were mostly Christians. It then became necessary for students of law to study the principles of divine right as taught in the Church, and while the books of the civil law were read by students for the priesthood, the Scriptures and the works of the Fathers were read by the students in law, thus blending the law of the two realms to some extent.(12)

10. *"Benefit of the Clergy," Ecclesiastical Court.*--As the old Roman Empire decayed and its power waned, the new one, "The Holy Roman Empire," gradually implanted itself in southwestern Europe. The humiliation that the divine law and the clergy suffered in being brought into the common courts gave rise to a system of courts within the Church for the purpose of enforcing her morals, doctrines, and discipline. Those courts were established in all Christian countries and had jurisdiction of all felonies excepting arson, treason, and a few other crimes that from time to time were put under the special jurisdiction of the state courts. Whenever a clergyman was arrested for a crime, he pleaded the "benefit of the clergy," and his case was transferred from the state court to the ecclesiastical court. Also, when a clergyman was convicted in the state court of any crime for which the punishment was death, he could plead the "benefit of the clergy," which was a protection against his execution.(13)

11. *Estates, Guardianship.*--Besides the jurisdiction already referred to, the ecclesiastical court had jurisdiction over the settlement of estates and the guardianship of children, which varied in different countries and was very indefinite in some of them.(14)

12. *Middle Ages, Common Law.*--During the Middle Ages there was a constant effort on behalf of the ecclesiastical courts to extend their jurisdiction, and a counter-effort on behalf of the state courts to assume jurisdiction of cases under the ecclesiastical law. In England, from the conquest of William the Conqueror to the Reformation, the extension of the jurisdiction of the ecclesiastical courts brought the new element of English common law into the canon law; and much of the canon law, following the jurisdiction assumed by the state courts, became the common law of the kingdom of England.(15)

13. *Gratian, Reformation.*--The canon law reached its full development in the twelfth century, when Gratian, the Blackstone of his age, compiled the system, but it subsequently lost its influence when the Reformation prevailed.(16)

14. *Bologna.*--The great school of jurisprudence, both of canon and civil law, was located at Bologna, Italy, which reached its zenith in the thirteenth century. To it students flocked from Western Europe, and from it were obtained the professors of law in the universities of England and other countries.(17)

15. *Church and State.*--In most of the Christian countries, the Church and State were united, and many of the judges in the civil courts were clergymen.(18)

16. *England, Roman Law.*--On account of England's being subject to Rome in its earliest age, and afterward because of its being conquered by France, the Roman law was pretty thoroughly intermixed with the native English law in the minor matters of the people, and governed in the more important ones.(19)

17. *America, English Law, Civil Law.*--The portions of America that were settled by the English, which included the original thirteen colonies, were under the English law. In Virginia the Episcopal Church, which was then the church of England, was made the church of state. Canada and that portion of the United States formerly known as Louisiana were governed by the civil law of France. Wherever the French government had no authority or civil officers, the government was directly under the missionaries of the Church.(20)

18. *Religious Tolerance, Established Church.*--The English law and English ideals prevailing in the original thirteen colonies,(21) there was a strong effort made by many of the delegates to the constitutional convention to have the Episcopal Church made the established church of the new republic. Thomas Jefferson and James Madison were probably the strongest opponents of the scheme, and outside of the great Carroll of Carrollton, they were the most earnest advocates of religious tolerance. The necessity for the fathers of this republic to be united, and their being unable to unite upon any church, caused the idea of an established church to be eliminated. Thus was established in our republic the freedom of conscience and the guarantee that no one shall be persecuted on account of his religious convictions.(22)

19. *Tribunals.*--The ecclesiastical courts as a part of the state system and the "benefit of the clergy," have been abolished in England and America. However, as we shall see further on, tribunals in the nature of the ecclesiastical court exist in churches and fraternities of all kinds in the United States.(23)

CHAPTER II.
WHAT IS A CHURCH?

20. *Church, Religious Society.*--Bouvier's definition of "Church" is: "A society of persons who profess a recognized religion." Chief Justice Shaw's definition is: "The church is neither a corporation nor a quasi-corporation, but a body of persons associated together for certain objects under the law. An aggregate body of individuals associated together in connection with a religious society. The term religious society may with propriety be applied in a certain sense to a church as that of religious association, religious union, or the like; yet in the sense church was and is used in our law, it is synonymous with parish or precinct and designates an incorporated society created and maintained for the support and maintenance of public worship. In this, its legal sense, a church is not a religious society. It is a separate body formed within such parish or religious society whose rights and usages are well known and to a great extent defined and established by law."(24)

21. *Doctrine, Constitution.*--A church in law is a mere fraternal organization. It may or may not have a written constitution, but it must have some central doctrine as its foundation or constitution.(25) Many of the Protestant denominations claim that the entire Bible is their constitution. The Jews may be said to consider the Old Testament as their constitution. All revealed truths may be said to be the constitution of the Catholic Church,(26) and when a doctrine concerning faith or morals is authoritatively declared by the Church to be a truth, it becomes a dogma.(27) The Apostles' Creed is an example of several dogmatic truths. The code of the Church is the Ten Commandments. A few sects, by a majority vote, make and change their constitutions at will.

22. *By-Laws.*--By-laws of the different religious organizations differ widely, from the decrees of the great councils of the Catholic Church down to the vote of the congregation of an independent denomination.

23. *Church, Religious Society.*--A church in one sense is more limited than a religious society; the latter comprehending all the members of the same faith. Even in the Catholic Church we hear of the Church of France, the Coptic Church, etc., spoken of in this sense. And in a still more limited sense we use the word as a synonym for parish. However, when the word "the" is used before church written with a capital letter, Catholics understand it to apply to the Roman Catholic Church in its entirety, while some non-Catholics apply it to Christendom.

24. *Church, Christians, Religion.*--The missions established in California prior to its admission into the Union were, in law, practically independent organizations and had no legal connection with the Church. Every society organized for the purpose of propagating the practice of religion may be a church in law.(28) The courts have made a distinction between Unitarians, who are considered Christians, and Deists, Theists, Free Religionists, and other infidels.(29) A sect or denomination without a given system of faith is not recognized as a religion in law.(30)

25. *Doctrine, Standard.*--To ascertain the tenets and doctrines of a church, resort must be had to history and to prior and contemporary standard writings of its members on theology.(31)

26. *Ecclesiastical Corporations, Religious, Quasi-public Corporations.*--Ecclesiastical corporations, in the sense in which the word is used in England, Germany, and France, are unknown to the United States, their places being supplied by religious societies or corporations considered as private bodies, in contradistinction to public or quasi-public corporations, such as towns, villages, cities, counties, and state. Therefore, the law of private corporations applies to religious societies and churches.

27. *Sect, Sectarianism.*--The Supreme Court of Nevada defines "sect" as follows: "A religious sect is a body or number of persons united in tenets, but constituting a distinct organization or party, by holding sentiments or doctrines different from those of other sects or people. In the sense intended in the constitution, every sect of that character is 'sectarian' and all members thereof are sectarians."(32) In Pennsylvania the court adopted the definitions given in the

Standard and in Webster's dictionaries.(33) The Supreme Court of Missouri, citing Webster's and the Century dictionaries, gave the following additional definition of sectarianism: "Sectarianism includes adherence to a distinct political party, as much as to a separate sect."(34) The Presbyterians(35) and the "Shakers"(36) have been adjudged sects.

28. *Sectarian.*--"Sectarian" has received more contradictory constructions than any other equally simple word in the English language. In Wisconsin the "King James" Bible was held to be a sectarian book;(37) but in Kentucky it was held that neither the Douay nor the "King James" Bible was a sectarian book.(38) The Missouri court extended sectarian so as to apply to the Republican party.(39) In Illinois an industrial school for girls in which the Catholic Sisters were employed as teachers, was held a sectarian institution;(40) while in Wisconsin, the "Wisconsin Industrial School for Girls," a private corporation organized and conducted by Protestant ladies, has received appropriations from the State and has had its reports published at state's expense, as a non-sectarian institution.(41) In New York the religious garb of the Catholic Sisters was practically decided to be sectarian;(42) but in Pennsylvania and Wisconsin it was decided that the dress of the Sisters was not sectarian.(43)

29. *Worship, Services, Mass.*--Any act of adoration, reverence, praise, thanks, honor, or veneration given to God, is religious worship.(44) A Sunday-school where the Bible was read and a hymn sung and a state temperance camp meeting where a prayer was said and hymns were sung, were held to be places of divine worship.(45) But a priest's house where he had a room fitted up for a chapel, was held to be not a place of worship.(46) It is very difficult to draw a line--no matter what curves you may give it--between the Protestant system of worship, which consists of the reading of the Bible, the singing of hymns, and the reciting of prayers, and such services in the public schools. Also, there would seem to be no *legal* difference between a prayer said or a hymn sung by a Catholic and a Protestant. As we have no established church in this country, we have no standard for prayers, hymns, or music.(47)

More solemn and impressive than her prayers adapted for schools is the Mass of the Catholic Church, defined thus: "The Mass is the unbloodied sacrifice of the body and blood of Christ."(48) It is defined in 26 Cyc, 940, as follows: "A religious ceremonial or observance of the Catholic Church;(49) a Catholic ceremonial celebrated by the priest in open church, where all who choose may be present and participate therein;(50) the sacrifice in the sacrament of the Eucharist or the consecration and oblation of the Host."(51)

30. *Parish.*--A parish has two meanings. In some States it is a minor division of public territory; but in States where there is no such division of territory, the State using instead "county" or "town," a parish rather applies to the people belonging to a particular church, who worship at a particular place. It is in the latter sense in which a parish should be construed in church law.(52)

Parishioner.--A parishioner must be defined in harmony with the meaning of the word "parish."(53)

31. *Clergyman.*--A clergyman is a man in holy orders or one who has been ordained in accordance with the rules of his church or denomination.(54)

32. *Minister.*--A minister is one who acts as, or performs some of the functions of, a clergyman.(55)

33. *Rector or Pastor.*--A rector or pastor is a clergyman who has charge of a parish.(56)

34. *Religion.*--Religion is still further distinguished, but not very satisfactorily defined, for the reason that etymologists have not agreed upon the derivation of the word. When the matter was brought before our courts and it became necessary to give a definition, the highest court in our country gave the following: "The term 'religion' has reference to one's views of his relations to his Creator, and to the obligations they impose of reverence for His being and character, and of obedience to His will. It is often confounded with *cultus* or form of worship of a particular sect, but it is distinguishable from the latter."(57) One of our highest courts held that "religion," as used in the trust provision in a will for the purchase and distribution of religious books or reading as they shall be deemed best, means "Christian."(58) But the Supreme Court of another State held that "religion" is not equivalent to "Christian" religion, but means the religion of any class of men.(59) Judge Willis defines "religion" thus: "It is what a man honestly believes in and approves of and thinks it his duty to inculcate on others whether with regard to this world or the next; a belief in any system of retribution by an overruling power. It must, I think, include the principle of gratitude to an active power who can confer blessings."(60)

CHAPTER III.

CONSTITUTIONAL LAW

35. *Religious Tests.*--The constitution of the United States provides that "no religious test shall ever be required as a qualification to any office or public trust under the United States."(61)

36. *Test Oath, Attainder.*--No test oath of any kind, whether religious or otherwise, can be required of a citizen of the United States. Therefore the test oath of Congress requiring an officer to swear that he never voluntarily bore arms against the United States, was held unconstitutional. Exclusion from any vocation on account of past conduct is punishment and contrary to the constitution on the subject of bills of attainder.(62) But there is a limitation to this rule to prevent the open violation of the laws of the United States or any State under the cloak of religion.(63)

37. *Establishment of Religion, Free Exercise.*--The first amendment to the United States constitution provides that "Congress shall make no law respecting an establishment of religion, or prohibiting the free exercise thereof."

38. *Sovereignty, States, Bigamy.*--The courts have held that this provision applies to Congress only, and can not be construed to interfere with the sovereignty of the several States; that the constitutional guarantee of religious freedom was not intended to prohibit legislation against polygamy; and that section 5352 of the United States Revised Statutes against bigamy, is constitutional. Also, that on a trial for bigamy in Utah, a man who was living in polygamy was not competent to serve as a juror.(64)

39. *Church of the Latter-Day Saints.*--In 1851 the assembly of the so-called State of Deseret, which subsequently became the territory of Utah, incorporated "the Church of the Latter-Day Saints." In 1887 Congress repealed the act of incorporation and abrogated the charter, which the Supreme Court held was within its plenary powers. The pretense of religious belief can not deprive Congress of the power to prohibit polygamy and all other open offenses against the enlightened sentiments of mankind.(65)

40. *Crime, Religion.*--The law prohibiting any person who is a polygamist or bigamist, or who teaches, advises, counsels, or encourages the same, from holding any office of honor, trust, or profit, is constitutional; and a crime is none the less so, nor less odious, because it is sanctioned by what any particular sect may designate as religion. A state has the right to legislate for the punishment of all acts inimical to the peace, good order, and morals of society.(66)

41. *Donation, Hostile, Religion.*--On the other hand the United States Supreme Court declared the legal right of donees of a college to make as a condition of the donation that all ecclesiastics, missionaries, and ministers of any sort, should be excluded from holding any station of duty in the college or even visiting the same. The condition being only negatively derogatory and hostile to the Christian religion, did not make the devise for the foundation of the college void.(67)

42. *Christian Scientist.*--A law requiring a person to be a physician to treat the sick, is constitutional; and the defense of a person who has no license to practice, that he is a Christian Scientist, is not good. Also, a parent must furnish a doctor for his sick child, notwithstanding that he believes in prayer cure.(68)

43. *Protestant.*--In the early days, under the constitution of the State, the courts of Massachusetts practically held that the Protestant religion was the religion of that State.(69) Also, the constitution of New Hampshire referred to different Christians, and the court in construing the terms "Roman Catholic" and "Protestant," held that any one who did not assent to the truth of Christianity as a distinct system of religion, could not be classed as either. The court stated that Mohammedans, Jews, pagans, and infidels, are neither "Catholics" nor "Protestants." The term "Protestant," as used in the constitution of New Hampshire, includes all Christians who deny the authority of the Pope of Rome. When the children of Protestant parents renounce that religion, and voluntarily accept another, they cease to be Protestants.(70) At present under the constitution of New Hampshire, the legislature may authorize towns or parishes to provide for the support of Protestant ministers.(71)

44. *Hospitals, Sisters, Appropriation.*--In 1864, Providence Hospital, of Washington, was incorporated by an act of Congress, for general hospital purposes. In 1897, $30,000 was appropriated for the District of Columbia to put up two isolation buildings in connection with two hospitals in that city, to be operated as a part of such hospitals. Providence Hospital was selected as one, and because it was in charge of Sisters of the Roman Catholic Church, the right of Congress to make the appropriation was disputed. Among other things, Judge Peackham says: "Whether the individuals who compose the corporation under its charter happen to be all Roman Catholics, or all Methodists, or all Presbyterians, or Unitarians, or members of any other religious organization, or of no organization at all, is of not the slightest consequence with reference to the law of its corporation, nor can the individual beliefs upon religious matters of the various incorporators be inquired into." The appropriation was "for two hospital buildings to be constructed in the discretion of the commissioners of the District of Columbia on the grounds of two hospitals and to be operated as a part of such hospitals."(72)

45. *Constitution, Rights.*--The provisions in the constitution do not in any way interfere with property rights obtained by a church organization prior to its adoption.(73)

46. *Aid, Contracts.*--Under the constitution of the United States, Congress cannot make appropriations for nor give aid to any denomination. Also, similar provisions are in many of the constitutions of the States. However, many cases arise out of contracts which border upon these various rules, and in some States the constitutional provision of the State is such that the State Legislature may legislate concerning religion and give certain aid and support thereto. Paying rent to a congregation for a school-room is not an appropriation or aid to a church contrary to the constitution.(74)

47. *Protestant Teacher, Tax.*--Formerly every parish in Massachusetts was obliged to elect and support a Protestant teacher, and might erect churches and parsonages. To provide the expenses thereof, a tax might be assessed upon the polls of the inhabitants.(75) Until 1890 New Hampshire permitted a tax to be levied in towns for religious purposes. It is still legal under the New Hampshire constitution to tax the inhabitants for the purpose of supporting Protestant teachers, but not to support a teacher of any other denomination.(76) A section of land in every township in Ohio was set apart for religious societies, in which they all shared equally.(77) Vermont had a similar provision.(78)

48. *Office, God.*--The constitutions of Arkansas, Mississippi, North Carolina, South Carolina, and Texas, prohibit a man from holding office who denies the existence of a Supreme Being; and the constitutions of Delaware, Maryland, Kentucky, and Tennessee, make all clergymen ineligible to hold a civil office.(79)

49. *Religious Liberty, Bible, Religious Garb, Wages.*--The authorities are not uniform as to what constitutes a violation of religious liberty. The question of whether the reading of the Bible in the public schools is a violation of the constitution, is an open one in some States and in others the courts have passed upon it, some holding that it is a violation of the constitution,(80) and some holding that it is not.(81) The weight of authority seems to permit the reading of the "King James" Bible,(82) and where portions only are read, as in "reading books" prepared for school work, or where the children are not obliged to be present during the exercises, the cases seem to be unanimous that it is not a violation of the constitution.(83) In Pennsylvania the court held that while Sisters in their religious garb might be teachers in the public schools, they could not give instruction in the Catholic religion at the schoolhouse before or after school hours, or at any other time use the school building for religious purposes. Also, in Wisconsin the court decided that while a portion of a parochial school building might be leased for public school purposes and the Sisters be employed therein as teachers, religious exercises and instructions could not be given in such leased premises.(84) In New York it was held not only that Sisters could not wear their religious garb or pray in school, but that they could not collect wages for teaching.(85)

Churches and State Law Considerations

A. CHURCH BYLAWS.

   1. By far, the most important legal document of any church is its bylaws. At a minimum, in addition to standard provisions relating to corporate procedure and structure, liability limiting provisions, federal tax provisions, the handling of contributions, etc., every church's bylaws should contain the following unique provisions, either by express statement or incorporation by reference to another organic document of the church:

   a. A statement of faith or a religious creed, stating with particularity the fundamental religious tenets of the organization.

   b. Procedures for, and qualifications of, the ordination of clergy.

   c. A statement of those ceremonies, rituals or practices considered to be sacramental (i.e., sacerdotal functions), and to what extent their exercise is restricted to ministers or other ordained persons.

2. Member discipline and/or removal provisions. It is common for nonprofit membership organizations to make provision for membership expulsion or termination, but churches often add some unique twists, usually related to religious/moral infractions. The legal consideration relates to the procedure by which termination is handled, rather than addressing the substantive bases for termination.

   a. Examine whether religious offenses are spelled out with particularity [OK] and whether there is a written record of interpretation/construction of language defining the offense [better], or whether offenses are vaguely defined, i.e., "any unbecoming conduct" [avoid] or there is no written record of interpretation [worse yet].

   b. Also examine whether members can be expelled based upon the mere determination of the minister [avoid] in his/her sole discretion [worse], or whether termination must be approved by a church committee [OK] or the governing board [better]. You may also insert a requirement that disciplinary hearings must be conducted in confidence and not broadcast to the church members or staff.

   c. Examine any differences between the way ministers are disciplined, if at all, and the way members are disciplined. It is common for ministerial conduct to be reviewed by a body composed of other ministers, whereas member conduct may be reviewed by lay persons. This is fine, but both procedures should have similar (though not necessarily the same) safeguards (review by peers, opportunity to answer charges, appeal to higher tribunal, etc.).

3. Examine the church structure as it relates to the division between temporal (legal) authority vs. ecclesiastical (religious) authority. Make sure the bylaws clearly identify which persons have what kind of authority. If anything, churches tend to think more about who has religious authority than legal authority, and the latter often gets ignored. Also, watch for anything that deprives the governing board for temporal concerns from having the final say as to any temporal matter (such as an ad hoc committee which can override the board, or boards which are merely advisory and must have their decisions approved by someone else). Every church corporation must have some body which, legally speaking, is the board of directors (although churches often call them something else), and that body must as a matter of law have the final say over temporal matters, or the board has abdicated its responsibility. In other words, make sure you know who the legal fiduciaries of the church are, and make sure they know who they are, and what it means to be a fiduciary.

B. CORPORATION LAWS.

1. Church corporations are governed generally by the state Nonprofit Corporation Acts, as are other nonprofit corporations. However, other more specialized state laws may also apply, for example:

   a. Church Trustee Corporation laws.

b. Ecclesiastical Corporation laws. Note: unlike general nonprofit corporations, which may be formed by one incorporator, ecclesiastical corporations are often required to have three (3) incorporators.

c. Many states have special (usually very old) statutes directed toward specific churches and/or denominations.

2. Church corporations often use specialized forms in connection with their Articles of Incorporation, such as in Michigan. California has a separate statute and forms for all religious corporations (not just churches). However, this is not true in all states.

3. Must a church corporation have voting members? The presumption may be yes, nonetheless many states allow a church to be formed as a directorship corporation.

C. PROPERTY TAX EXEMPTION.

1. Not all states have property tax exemption statutes specifically addressed to ecclesiastical organizations. For example, Michigan law provides exemptions for:

a. Property "owned and occupied by nonprofit charitable institutions incorporated under the laws of this state with the buildings and other property thereon while occupied by them solely for the purposes for which they were incorporated." A charitable institution includes an ecclesiastical organization, so long as the other requirements of the statute are satisfied.

b. "Houses of public worship, with the land on which they stand, the furniture therein and all rights in the pews, and any parsonage owned by a religious society of this state and occupied as a parsonage are exempt." A religious society includes an ecclesiastical organization, but on the other hand, is not limited to a traditional church.

c. Note: Since neither of these exemptions is specifically directed towards ecclesiastical organizations, neither exemption is limited to organizations which hold themselves out to the public as a church. Thus, even the "house of public worship" exemption may be available to non-church ("para-church") religious organizations. Laws in other states will vary considerably.

2. Caveat: In many states, when any real property exempt from taxation is leased or used by a private individual, association, or corporation for a for-profit business purpose, the lessees or users of this real property shall be subject to taxation in the same amount and to the same extent as though the lessee or user were the owner of this real property. In other words, mere ownership of property by a religious organization is often not enough to make the property tax exempt - it must also be used for a tax exempt purpose.

3. Caveat: The determination of whether property is used for an exempt purpose for property tax purposes is often made independent of federal tax exempt status. Why? Because

property tax exemptions are governed by state law, determined by state bodies, and decided based on state case precedent, etc. Do not think that federal tax exemption by itself will go very far in establishing a state property tax exemption.

D. UNEMPLOYMENT COMPENSATION.

1. "Employment" for purposes of many state acts includes service performed by an individual in the employ of a religious, charitable, educational, or other organization exempt from tax under IRC §501(c)(3).

2. However, in most states, "employment" does not include service performed either:

a. "In the employ of a church or a convention or association of churches or an organization that is operated primarily for religious purposes and is operated, supervised, controlled, or principally supported by a church or a convention or association of churches"; or

b. "By an ordained, commissioned, or licensed minister of a church in the exercise of the ministry or by a member of a religious order in the exercise of duties required by the order."

c. A notable exception is New York, which covers all religious organization employees under its unemployment compensation act.

3. Definitions of terms. In keeping with federal precedents:

a. Church, convention of churches, and association of churches are interchangeable terms denoting that every ecclesiastical organization is intended to be included, regardless of the form of its ecclesiastical structure.

b. Church controlled organizations, such as a church camp or church school, can qualify for treatment as a church.

c. Ordained, commissioned and licensed are interchangeable terms denoting that every minister is to be treated equally, regardless of the ecclesiastical form of recognition as a minister.

d. A member of a religious order is treated the same as a minister, even though he/she is not a "minister," and even though a religious order is not the same as a church. [There are more religious orders in existence than you might think.]

E. SALES TAXES.

1. In many states, purchases of tangible personal property by an ecclesiastical organization may be exempt from sales tax either as:

    a. a regularly organized church or house of religious worship; or

    b. a recognized IRC §501(c)(3) or §501(c)(4) organization.

    c. A notable exception is California, which does not base its sales tax exemptions on the nature or character of the organization at all, but exempts only certain kinds of transactions. In other words, there is no blanket exemption for religious organizations.

2. In states where religious organizations are exempted, normally sales tax exemptions do not apply to:

    a. activities that are mainly commercial enterprises (including UBIT or unrelated business income generating activities); or

    b. purchases of certain kinds of vehicles.

3. Ecclesiastical organizations are normally not exempt from charging sales tax on retail sales to others - but again, this will vary considerably from state to state.

F. DISSOLUTION.

1. Churches are exempt in most states from needing to obtain the consent of the Attorney General in the event of a dissolution. However, in a few states it is still advisable to get a letter from the AG's office stating its consent is not required (just to keep in your file).

2. Churches are not exempt from needing to file a Certificate of Dissolution and/or to receive a Certificate of Tax Clearance from the appropriate state agencies.

G. CHARITABLE SOLICITATIONS ACT.

1. In nearly every state, the Charitable Solicitations Act does not apply to "duly constituted religious organizations or a group affiliated with and forming an integral part of a religious organization no part of the net income of which inures to the direct benefit of any individual if it has received a declaration of current tax exempt status from the United States" or equivalent language.

2. Every ecclesiastical organization should satisfy the definition in the preceding paragraph. But query: What about a church which has not "received a declaration of current tax exempt status from the United States" because it is mandatorily exempted from having to do so?

CHAPTER IV.

STATUTORY LAW

50. *Wisconsin, Mississippi, New York.*--The statutory law of the different States of the Union is so varied and the laws of one State are of so little interest to the people of another that it would be almost useless and beyond the boundaries of this work to give the substance of the various statutes. In some States there is a limitation upon the real estate that a church or charitable organization may hold, and in other States there is no limitation whatever. Wisconsin, perhaps, occupies the extreme of greatest liberality, by not only allowing full freedom in everything relating to religion and charity, but it further excepts from the limitation all rights of alienation of real estate granted or devised to a charitable association or to literary or charitable corporations organized under the law of the State. The State of Mississippi probably stands at the other extreme both in the narrowness of its constitution and statutory law, and prohibits any devise or bequest of any personal property or real estate in favor of any religious or ecclesiastical corporation or any religious or ecclesiastical society. Neither does it exempt a clergyman, physician, or lawyer, from examination as a witness concerning information that he obtained in the performance of his functions or duties as such. Its judges, however, are more liberal than its legislators, and I know of no instance in which a clergyman, physician, or lawyer, as a witness, was sent to jail for contempt of court for not divulging information obtained in his professional capacity. Probably New York has the most complete code(86) relating to religious corporations.

51. *Real Estate, Parish, Diocese, Taxation.*--It is very important that a congregation about to purchase real estate should examine and understand the statutory law of the State governing the powers and authority of the Church as a civil organization. In some States there is no special law for incorporating religious societies; while in most States there are special provisions therefor. For this reason, I emphasize the fact that no parish or clergyman is justified in organizing a congregation or purchasing land without first knowing the law of that particular State. But generally it is best that each congregation be incorporated and that its property be held in the name of the corporation, so that the debts of one corporation will not embarrass the diocese, and that bequests and gifts made to a church may be enforced in the courts. The proceedings to incorporate are fully stated in the statutes of each State. One of the things of the utmost importance is that any notice to be given must be given strictly as required by law.(87) Another is to incorporate in the way that avoids taxation.(88)

52. *Riot, Damages.*--Under a statute providing that a person whose property is destroyed by riot may bring suit against the county for damages, a corporation for religious purposes, as well as an individual, has a right of action.(89)

53. *Use, Change, Parsonage, Discipline, Doctrine, Curate.*--When a fee simple is acquired by a religious corporation, without restriction as to quantity, but limiting the purpose of its use, a subsequent Legislature, with the consent of the corporation, has power to change or abrogate altogether the restrictions as to the use of the land.(90) And the Legislature may empower the church corporation to convey a house devised to it for a parsonage with a condition that it be kept in repair, and invest the proceeds in other property to be held for the same purpose. (91) A State legislature can not interfere in church discipline and doctrine, as by legislating what shall constitute a curate in the Catholic Church.(92)

CHAPTER V.

UNINCORPORATED CHURCH SOCIETIES

54. *Partners, Debt, Liability.*--Where several go into an undertaking without first being incorporated they are usually liable as partners, each one being responsible for the whole debt. In some States the same liability exists where an attempt has been made to incorporate, but there was a failure to comply fully with the law.(93) There is some authority freeing the individual members of a religious society from liability for the debts of such society,(94) and holding that an agent of such society could not bind the society in their associated capacity by a promissory note,(95) but the rule is that the members of an unincorporated society who actively incur lawful debts or ratify them after their creation are personally liable. There are exceptions to this rule by statute or decisions in a few States.(96) Also, the law of personal liability is settled in England.(97)

55. *Pastor, Salary.*--In a late case in Wisconsin where a pastor had a contract with his congregation as to his salary, after the clergyman's death his heirs recovered the unpaid part of his salary in an action against a few of the individual members of the congregation.(98)

56. *Building, Materials.*--The members of the building committee of an unincorporated church are liable for materials purchased by them for the church, notwithstanding that the seller charged the materials in the name of the church, and that at the time that the purchase was made, he was told that the money for payment was to be raised by subscription among the congregation.(99)

57. *Management, Disability.*--An unincorporated society is managed by those who are competent to transact their own business. Therefore, it would seem that members must be men over twenty-one years of age, and not under legal disability. The minor sons in a family who have continued their attendance at the religious services until of full age, are considered members.(100)

58. *Shakers, Sect, Catholic Church, Trustees, Funds.*--Although the sect called Shakers is not incorporated, yet it has been allowed to take and hold property for church purposes.(101) In Massachusetts, by statute, a sect may take and hold property for religious purposes without incorporation.(102) The Roman Catholic Church is a recognized public corporation by most nations, including the United States.(103) No individual member of any such body has any title to the lands it holds, but the lands are the property of the society in its aggregate capacity.(104) After property has been acquired, the trustees have no right to distribute it among the members, as such power could not be conferred upon them by a majority vote even when approved by an order of the court. The contributors did not intend their funds to be so disposed of, and if they failed to attain the use intended, they must be returned to the donors, and if not called for, would escheat to the state.(105) Where an unincorporated society has purchased property and taken the title thereto in the name of one of its members, when it subsequently incorporates such member may be required to execute a conveyance to the corporation.(106)

59. *Contract, Binding.*--Persons forming a religious society may make a contract for the support of its minister by a majority vote.(107) When such unincorporated society by a majority vote enters into a contract or compromises a suit, it is binding upon the minority.(108)

60. *Court, Trust.*--Any member of an unincorporated society may go into a court of equity on behalf of himself and others to enforce the execution of a trust in favor of the society.(109)

61. *Societies, Membership, Forfeiture.*--Voluntary religious societies when not restricted by their charters or articles of association, may make by-laws declaring what shall constitute membership and what shall operate as a forfeiture thereof, applicable to existing as well as to future members. Where money is voted to be raised by an assessment to be made at a subsequent period, a person who was a member of the religious society at the time that such vote was passed, but withdraws before the time of assessment, is not liable to taxation.(110)

CHAPTER VI.

INCORPORATED RELIGIOUS SOCIETIES

62. *Special Law, General Laws.*--In most of the States there is a special law under which congregations may be incorporated. New York is a good example.(111) Where such law does not exist, the congregation may be incorporated under the general laws. For business reasons each congregation should be incorporated.(112)

63. *Officers, Discipline, Property.*--When a church society incorporates it becomes a private corporation, and the officers are bound to manage the property in the most upright and careful manner according to the discipline of the church.(113) When a parish incorporates, the title to the parish property vests in the corporation, to which trustees may be compelled to convey it.(114)

64. *Incorporation, Evidence.*--The certificate of incorporation or charter of a religious society or a certified copy thereof from the public record, is the proper evidence thereof.(115) Secondary evidence and evidence *aliunde* may be competent in some forums.(116) In most States if incorporation is alleged in the complaint, it need not be proved unless denied by an affidavit or a verified answer.

65. *Congregation, Members.*--The act of incorporation applies only to the particular congregation petitioning for it and does not extend to other churches, even though they are a subsequent growth within the same territory.(117) Incorporation once established is presumed to continue.(118) When a new religious society is formed and incorporated, consisting of individuals from existing parishes, the members of the new society from the time of its incorporation cease to be members of the respective parishes to which they had belonged.(119)

66. *Temporal Affairs, Management.*--A majority of a religious corporation at a regularly called meeting may, by a vote taken, bind the minority in all temporal affairs.(120) The character of membership in the religious corporation may be very different from that of membership in the church.(121) The fact that a member has been declared out of the church by an ecclesiastical tribunal, may not affect his rights in the management of the temporal concerns of the corporation.(122)

67. *Corporators, Change.*--In isolated cases here and there it has been held that a majority of the corporators of a religious society has the right to change the form of church government, as from the Congregational Church to an organization in connection with the Presbyterian Church.(123) But it is a general rule that a majority of the congregation can act only consistently with the particular and general laws of the church organization, but not in violation of them.(124)

68. *Constitution, Subsequent Laws.*--An ecclesiastical society formed before the adoption of the state constitution is not by that constitution and subsequent laws concerning religious societies divested of its legal character.(125)

69. *Name, Change.*--The name of an ecclesiastical corporation is arbitrary and a change or alteration in its name does not affect its identity.(126) A charter will not be granted to a church with a name so like another church in the same State, that one may be taken for the other.(127)

70. *Church, Regular.*--In church organizations those who adhere to the regular order of the church, legal and general, though a minority, are the true congregation and constitute the corporation if incorporated.(128)

71. *Notice, Legal.*--All the proceedings of a corporation, including notice, must be in accordance with the constitution and by-laws, and no business transacted contrary thereto is legal.(129)

72. *Control, Secede, Vested Rights.*--The officers of a church corporation have control of the business management for all civil purposes, excepting as otherwise provided by the articles of organization, charter, or by-laws of the corporation. However, the by-laws must not contravene the laws of the State.(130) A charter was refused in Pennsylvania which provided that the congregation might, by a majority vote, dissolve or secede from the central body and divide the property. (131) A charter of incorporation may be amended in harmony with the principles, discipline, and objects of the church, but not otherwise.(132) The fact that incorporation of a church confers certain rights and privileges under the charter, such charter being accepted, does not give the church corporation any vested rights.(133)

73. *Consolidation, Control, Dissolution.*--So far as the State law is concerned, two different denominations may form one corporation;(134) or two or more congregations of the same organization may form one corporation.(135) Where such consolidation is attempted, the new organization must have control of all the property.(136) So long as different congregations attempting to consolidate retain their respective identities, they do not form a single corporation.(137) It is a general rule that a corporation may be dissolved by taking the steps required by law. As there are various statutory provisions in the different States, each case had best be attended to by an attorney. In some States there is a provision that where a corporation fails to carry out its functions for a stated time, it thereby becomes dissolved. The omission of a parish for one year to elect officers, does not necessarily operate as a dissolution under such statute. In case of dissolution under a statute of that kind, the property of the church is not forfeited to the State.(138)

74. *Debt, Limited.*--The amount of debt which the trustees of a religious society may be authorized to create, may be limited by its constitution.(139)

75. *Conditions, Effect.*--Where $1,000 was given defendants to erect and maintain forever a Lutheran church and prohibiting the grantee from alienating or disposing of or otherwise changing or encumbering the land by deed, a mortgage given to secure a legitimate debt was held valid, as the legal title was in the corporation and a court of equity could not refuse to enforce the mortgage for the payment of an honest debt under color of protecting a charitable use.(140) But property given a congregation for the maintenance of a church that becomes dissolved, reverts to the heirs as a resulting trust.(141) A corporation that has been authorized to purchase land may execute a mortgage for the purchase money or a part of it without further authority.(142) Where by an ancient agreement a meeting-house was to remain in a particular place, a vote of the congregation will not justify pulling it down, and an action of trespass will lie for razing it and damages will be given for the value of the building.(143)

76. *Suits, Parties.*--When a church is incorporated, it should be sued in its corporate name; but when the bishop of the Catholic church holds the legal title to the land in litigation, he should be made a party.(144) And if there are two sets of officers contending for control, service of the papers upon the intruders may not be sufficient. The safer practice is to serve upon both.(145) A suit by the trustees of a religious society to restrain other parties claiming to be trustees from interfering in the management and control of the society property, is properly brought in the corporate name of the trustees and not in the name of the State.(146)

77. *Incorporation, Sufficient.*--Where the articles of incorporation were drawn and signed in the form required by law, excepting as to the acknowledgment, and were recorded, and the corporation organized in good faith, it became a DE *facto* corporation and was sufficient to entitle it to sue to prevent certain members from perverting the use of its property.(147)

78. *Dissolution, Fund.*--The corporation of a congregation can not by seceding and a majority vote dissolve the corporation where it is a part of a superior body. (148) But the courts have plenary powers over corporations under the United States jurisdiction, such as territories, and may dissolve a corporation.(149) The fact that the dissolution is contrary to, or authorized by church discipline, makes no difference as to granting the dissolution, as such discipline can not supersede the state law.(150) On dissolution of a religious corporation, the surplus fund derived from a legacy should be disposed of in the manner the court believes to be most in harmony with the will of the contributors to the fund, could they have foreseen the event.(151)

79. *Reorganization.*--A church corporation may reorganize and be reinstated into all rights that it formerly had.(152) The steps to be taken to reorganize are usually provided by statute and should be closely followed. Upon the reorganization, the old corporation becomes terminated.(153)

80. *Meetings, Majority, Quorum.*--In corporate meetings, meetings of boards, and meetings of committees duly called, a majority vote of those present determines the action of the body. If the membership is indefinite, those who attend such meeting constitute a quorum; but if the membership is definite, it requires a majority of the voting members to constitute a quorum, unless the law of the State or the constitution (articles of organization) or by-laws provide a different number.(154)

CHAPTER VII.

SUPERIOR AUTHORITY

81. *Protestant, Ministers, Bishop.*--In most church organizations the authority is divided into superior and inferior. In countries where there is an established Protestant church, the superior authority is first in the king and queen and secondly in the bishops. The inferior authority is in the ministers and secular officers of the church. Where there is no established church, the synod or bishop is the superior authority. Thus decisions of our courts usually apply to all churches alike.

82. *Roman Catholic Church, Pope, Bishops, Delegated.*--In the Roman Catholic Church the superior authority is first in the Pope and secondly in the other bishops. This superior authority is graded and some of it may be delegated, as in case of a Papal delegate. But the general rule that delegated authority can not be again delegated by the delegate without special authority applies to church matters.

83. *Bishop, Discipline, Clergy.*--Within his diocese the bishop is the executive officer, the legislature, and the judiciary; but he is subject to the superior authority of the Church. The bishop may make laws for his diocese, subject to the limitation of the general doctrine and discipline of the Church. He has original jurisdiction of all causes arising in his diocese, and may decide them in the first instance and inflict such penalties, suspension, or excommunication, in accordance with the canons of the Church, as he deems fit. The clergy are subject to his orders and discipline according to the canon law. However, without special contract, the bishop is not civilly liable for the salary of a priest under him, either while he is actually in the line of his assigned duties or while waiting to be assigned.(155)

84. *Local, Secular Matters.*--There is still another division of superior and inferior authority: the local corporation or congregation has nothing whatever to do with the doctrinal or disciplinary functions of the Church; but has only such powers and authority with regard to secular matters as is provided by the laws of the State or conferred by the articles of organization, charter, and by-laws. Also, unless there is some other rule to the contrary, only the male members who are over twenty-one years of age, have a voice and vote in such corporation.(156)

85. *Unincorporated, Authority.*--When a church is not incorporated, all its elections and proceedings, so far as they are not contrary to the laws of the State, must be in accordance with the rules and regulations of the Church; and the rule that the inferior authority must give way to the superior authority in all matters within the limitations of the constitution and laws of the organization, prevails.(157) However, courts are not always clear on the last part of this rule.(158)

86. *Tribunal, Action, Appeal.*--When any question arises and is being adjudicated in the tribunal of the church organization, either as an original action or on appeal, the State court will not interfere so long as the proceedings are in accordance with the rules and regulations of the church, unless some vested right to property is in question or some one's right as a citizen of the State or of the United States is being infringed.(159)

87. *Spiritual Authority, Excommunication.*--Neither the Pope nor the bishop has any but spiritual authority within the State.(160) The law of this country considers excommunication as expelling from membership; but does not tolerate interference with civil or property rights of citizens. Therefore, major excommunication *non tolerati*, is unlawful in the United States.(161) However, a bishop is not liable for any expression of his opinion as to the extent of his episcopal authority nor for any act of omission in the exercise of his spiritual functions.(162) The civil courts will not go behind a church authority to inquire as to excommunication, but may examine as to the competency of the tribunal according to the laws of the denomination.(163)

88. *Constitution, Limited, Decisions.*--A written constitution is not necessary to prove the connection between a subordinate and superior ecclesiastical body; but it will be inferred from the circumstances of the case.(164) The superior may dissolve or reorganize an inferior body as a congregation.(165) In fact the superior authority, in religious matters, is plenary, excepting as limited by the laws of the State and the constitution of the Church.(166) The decisions of the ecclesiastical tribunals in all cases on doctrine, order, and discipline, are conclusive in the state courts.(167)

CHAPTER VIII.

INFERIOR AUTHORITY

89. *Priesthood, Discipline.*--The inferior authority in the Church may be said to be in the priesthood, whose rights and duties are fixed by the canon law, but who are still further subject to the reasonable diocesan rules made by the bishop. The disciplinary relation of a priest to his bishop is substantially the same as that of a captain to his colonel, and implicit obedience in accordance with the discipline of the Church may be strictly enforced by the bishop in so far as it relates to ecclesiastical matters, including doctrine and discipline, in which the priest can not resort to the courts of the State, but must submit to the tribunals of the church.(168)

90. *Congregation, Insubordinate, Discipline.*--The male members of a congregation are invested with no visitorial or controlling power, but only such authority as is given under the laws of incorporation.(169) Where an inferior organization, as a congregation, refuses to receive a clergyman appointed by the bishop, it is an act of insubordination to the ecclesiastical authority of the Church and in violation of its discipline, which authorizes the issuing of a peremptory mandamus commanding them to admit the clergyman.(170)

91. *Pastor, Parish, Relation.*--When a clergyman's connection with a church had been duly dissolved, he ceased to be pastor of the church and an arrangement with the parish to retain his relation as pastor of such church was nugatory and void.(171)

92. *Clergymen, Citizens.*--Clergymen residing in an incorporated town are not exempt from the performance of any duties required of citizens, unless such exemption is given by statute.(172)

93. *Doctrine and Discipline, Authority.*--In all matters concerning doctrine and discipline of the Church, the inferior authority, such as ministers, priests, and deacons, as well as the congregation, must submit to the decision of the higher authority, whether bishop, synod, or council.(173)

94. *Sect, Suit, Property.*--A number of people formed a congregation and became incorporated in 1810, the members being mostly of Presbyterian extraction. This independent congregation bought and paid for property, the title vesting in the corporation. In 1811 the congregation passed resolutions unanimously that it "would be imprudent and unscriptural" to establish a new religious sect, and voted to join the First Reformed Dutch Church, which had an organization of inferior and superior authority. The congregation was received into and became a part of the general organization, and remained so until 1860, when a majority of the congregation voted to employ a Methodist minister, and when his name was submitted to the superior authority, the "classes," he was rejected as not belonging to the church. Then by a majority vote, the congregation seceded and assumed its first name, and thereafter brought suit for the church property. The court held that by joining the First Reformed Dutch Church, the title of the property vested in the congregation of that church as represented by its corporation, and that when the majority seceded and left the church, they had no right nor title to any of the property. And the court laid down the general rule that a majority of a church congregation may direct and control any church matters consistently with the particular and general laws of the organization or denomination to which it belongs, but not in violation of them. (174)

95. *Priest, Salary.*--The fact that a bishop who holds the title to all the diocesan property in his own name in trust appoints a priest to the parish or as chaplain to a hospital, does not give the priest a right of action against the bishop personally for his salary. The relation of bishop and priest is not that of employer and employe, but is that of ecclesiastical superior and inferior.(175)

96. *Curate, Induction, Rector.*--The *jus patronatus* of the Spanish law has been abrogated in Louisiana. The wardens of the church can not compel a bishop to institute a curate of their appointment, nor is he in any sense subordinate in his clerical functions to the wardens of any church within his diocese.(176) In the absence of a positive rule of the ecclesiastical body, no ceremony of induction is necessary for the rector of a parish.(177) A clergyman appointed "permanently" to a rector ship holds it for an indefinite period during the pleasure of the contracting parties, and either of the contracting parties may give the other notice of termination, and with the concurrence of the higher ecclesiastical authority of the diocese, a change may be made.(178) It is doubtful, however, whether in most States a permanent appointment would not be construed as a contract for life, determinable only for good cause.(179)

97. *Controversy, Tribunal, Decision.*--When the clergyman and his parishioners submit a controversy to an ecclesiastical tribunal, the decision, if not impeached for good cause, is justification in the party conforming to it.(180) And a minister who submits to a church tribunal and is ousted after fair hearing and trial, can not obtain a writ of mandamus from the civil court to compel his reinstatement.(181) Also, after a minister has been dismissed in due manner by the tribunal of his denomination, the civil court will enjoin him from usurping his office.(182)

98. *Priest, Dwelling, Servant.*--A Catholic priest in charge of a congregation at the will of the bishop and occupying a dwelling-house belonging to the church, is a servant and not a tenant, and his right to occupancy ceases with his services. (183) The law is different with regard to a Methodist minister who is in charge of his parish by an annual conference and can not be ejected by the congregation or bishop until the next conference, as he has possession of the church property without superior authority.(184)

99. *Injunction, Bishop, Priest, Trial.*--On application for an injunction to restrain the bishop from passing a sentence against a priest, the only ground on which a court can exercise jurisdiction is that the threatened action of the bishop will affect the civil rights of the priest.(185) A bishop can not remove a priest without an accusation, hearing, or trial, and forbid him to exercise any priestly function where such removal would cut off the priest's income and destroy his means of living in his vocation.(186) However, in the same case it was held that a complaint stating that the bishop failed and neglected to assign the plaintiff to the exercise of his office of priest in said diocese to the plaintiff's damage, etc., failed to show that any right of property or civil right was involved and the priest was non-suited, while in the former case an injunction was issued against the bishop. (187)

100. *Confession, Privacy, Authority.*--A Catholic priest, although about to administer an office of his religion to a sick person at the latter's request, has no legal authority, by virtue of his priestly character, to forcibly remove from the room a person lawfully there.(188)

101. *Debts, Permission, Presumed.*--Notwithstanding a rule or ecclesiastical law of the church that a pastor shall not contract debts in the name or for the sake of the church without the written permission of the bishop, such written permission is not evidence that debts contracted under it are the legal debts of the bishop. The authority which bishops delegate to priests is under the ecclesiastical law and prima facia ecclesiastical authority, and must be presumed to be so in the absence of all evidence to the contrary.(189)

102. *Official Acts, Subscriptions.*--The official acts of a minister coming in question incidentally, unless contrary to the statute, are as valid as the official acts of any other officer.(190) A clergyman who was engaged to conduct dedication services and was requested by the officers of the local corporation to solicit subscriptions for paying off the indebtedness of the church, but was not appointed agent to receive such subscriptions, had no authority to accept a subscription for the corporation.(191)

103. *Exemptions, Clergy.*--The exemptions given ministers by the statutes of some States are liberally construed.(192) Without any statutory exemption, the clergy are liable for all duties required of other citizens.(193)

104. *Minister, Contributions, Deposed.*--No religious teacher or minister can be enjoined from receiving voluntary contributions, although he has been deposed by some ecclesiastical tribunal.(194)

105. *Fees, Usages, Excess.*--The fees of a priest of the Catholic Church are regulated by the laws and usages of that Church, and where in this country the pew rent and collections go for the support of the priest and the current church expenses, a priest is not accountable for the excess of such collections over these expenditures.(195)

106. *Salary, Fees.*--Under the act of March, 1814, incorporating a congregation, the congregation, being the legal owners and temporal administrators of the property which it was authorized to hold, had the exclusive power to fix the salary of the parish priest or the tariff of fees for marriages, burial, etc. No such power could be exercised under that act by the Pope or any bishop.(196)

107. *Clergyman, Salary.*--Where a clergyman agreed with a congregation that the salary should be what could be raised by subscription, the congregation was bound to use due diligence in procuring subscriptions, and as it did so, that was all that the clergyman could recover.(197)

108. *Curate, Services.*--In an action by a curate against a religious corporation for personal services, the court will not inquire into the spiritual relations existing between the parties, but will examine their legal rights only.(198)

109. *Minister, Dismissal, Money Advanced.*--After a parish has voted to dismiss the minister, it is not competent to prove irregular conduct or immorality in answer to his claim for salary, without alleging it in the vote of dismissal.(199) In Illinois it was held that a priest who advanced money from his private resources for improving church property, had an equitable lien upon the property for all the money advanced, with legal interest.(200) But in Pennsylvania, where a priest under the direction of the bishop built a church in his parish for mission purposes, and in doing so expended some of his own money, it was held that in the absence of proof of any rule or custom of the Catholic Church making the payment of such expenses obligatory on the parish, that he could not recover the money so expended from his congregation.(201)

CHAPTER IX.

MEMBERSHIP

110. *Business, Religious Membership.*--Unless there is some other law or rule to the contrary, the male members of the congregation over twenty-one years of age constitute the business membership of a religious society.(202) But the question of membership of religious societies or congregations is left to be determined by the rules of the religious denomination to which they belong.(203) And where a condition of membership is that the person must contribute to the support of the church and be a communicant, if he is not a communicant he is not entitled to vote.(204)

111. *Regular, Doctrines, Support.*--The ones who adhere and submit to the regular order and doctrines of the church, although a minority, constitute the true congregation.(205) At least two things must concur to qualify a person as a voter: first, stated attendance at divine worship in the congregation; and, second, contribution to the support of the church.(206) The list of members kept by the clerk or secretary of the congregation is evidence of membership.(207) A person who denies any part of the system of theology received and taught by the denomination is not a member of the church.(208)

112. *Factions, Authority.*--Where two factions of a church, each claiming to be the church, try members of the other faction, a court may determine which of the factions is the authorized authority or that the action taken by either or both of them is nugatory for want of authority.(209)

113. *Faith, Burial.*--Whether a person died in the faith of the Roman Catholic Church so as to be entitled to burial in its cemetery, is not a question within the jurisdiction of civil courts, but must be decided by the ecclesiastical authorities. (210)

114. *Rules, Membership.*--Every denomination has the right to prescribe by rules, its constitution, or its by-laws, the conditions of membership; and any one who will not subscribe to and practice the doctrines of the denomination is not a member.(211)

115. *Minor.*--Where the legal members of a society that is incorporated consist of male members of the church of full age, when minor sons become of age, they become legal members of the corporation, provided they remain in the church. (212)

116. *Officers, Non-Members.*--It has been held that a person may be an officer or member of the church corporation or its temporal concerns without being a member of the denomination.(213)

117. *Debts, Unincorporated Parish.*--In Connecticut members of an ecclesiastical society formed by voluntary association under the statutes of the State are not individually liable for the debts of such society.(214) But where there is no statute on the subject, the members of an unincorporated parish are liable for lawful debts contracted or ratified by them, and their property may be levied on for such debts incurred or judgments rendered while they are members of the society.(215) The members of an unincorporated parish may be sued to recover the salary of a deceased pastor up to the time of his death.(216)

118. *Execution, Property.*--While an execution against a territorial parish may be levied on the property of a member of the parish, it can not be levied on property of a person who ceased to be a member before the levy.(217)

119. *Incorporated, Subscriptions.*--The members of an incorporated poll parish are not individually liable on a judgment and execution against the corporation, excepting on the unpaid subscriptions.(218)

120. *Expelled, Merits.*--Mandamus can not be resorted to to restore a member regularly expelled from his church, as a court will not inquire into the merits of the case.(219)

121. *Lay Members, Appointed.*--Where the statute provides that two lay members of the corporation of a Catholic parish shall be appointed annually "by the committee of the congregation," the members of the congregation have no right to elect said two members, and those appointed in the proper manner are lawful officers.(220)

CHAPTER X.

HERESY AND SECESSION

122. *Mother Church, Control.*--A majority of the members of a congregation can not by their vote leave the church and transfer the property of the congregation to another church so long as any portion of the congregation remains faithful to the mother church of which such congregation forms a part. Such minority shall retain control of the property.(221)

123. *Seceders, Funds.*--Nor can seceders from a religious denomination retain the funds in their hands as trustees on the ground that they were members of the society when the funds accrued.(222) The title to church property in a divided congregation is in that part of the congregation which is acting in harmony with its own law; and the ecclesiastical laws and principles which were accepted among them before the dispute began are the standards for determining which party is right.(223)

124. *Society, Foreign Language, Independent.*--The formation of a society distinct from the rest of the congregation for the purpose of instruction in a portion of the doctrine of the same church in a foreign language is not a separation from the congregation, although it has its own minister and officers.(224) Where an independent congregation of one denomination votes unanimously to go over to another denomination, and the title to the church property is in the parish corporation, the seceders take with them the church property.(225)

125. *Subordinate, Incorporated.*--A religious society subordinate to church judicature's, which declares itself independent and becomes incorporated under the general law of the state and subsequently purchases land and takes title in the name of the corporation, holds such land independently of such church judicatures.(226)

126. *"Church," Seceders, Debt.*--Where a religious society amended its constitution as provided therein, those who adhered to the amended constitution constituted the "church," and those who refused to do so were seceders.(227) After seceding, a member of a parish is liable for a debt existing at the time of his secession.(228)

127. *Bible, Constitution, Withdrawal.*--A religious organization that takes the Bible as its constitution can not declare a member a seceder who interprets it contrary to the Augsburg Confession of the denomination.(229) What amounts to a voluntary withdrawal of members from a religious association, is a question of law.(230)

128. *Majority, Obligation.*--The fact that a majority of the members of a religious corporation secede therefrom by a vote, does not affect its obligation entered into prior thereto.(231) Two factions of a church separating and keeping up different organizations may both still retain their membership in the denomination.(232)

129. *Division, Funds.*--Where there is a division in a denomination by the secession of a part of the members from the mother church, the Legislature has no authority to divide the funds and give a part to the seceding division.(233)

130. *Methodist, Slave holding, Non-Slave holding, Quarrel, Schism, Secession.*-- The division of the Methodist church into distinct organizations of slave holding and non-slave holding States, was not a secession and neither division lost its interest in the common property.(234) A quarrel in a congregation growing out of an illegal election followed by the majority excluding the minority from the church, is not a schism, and is no ground for a division of the church property.(235) The secession of a whole congregation does not carry with it the church property; and those who are left and adhere to the mother church retain control of the property. (236) When the seceders from one church join another, they forfeit all claim to any interest held by the former and lose identity with it.(237)

CHAPTER XI.

EXCOMMUNICATION

131. *Definitions, Minor.*--Excommunication, as construed in law, is the official announcement by the superior authority of the termination of membership in a religious body and the forfeiture of spiritual privileges of the church. It is one of the methods of discipline in the nature of expulsion from membership in a fraternity, and the fact of expulsion from a church is conclusive proof that the person expelled is not a member of such church. Whether the excommunication was wrong or not can not be examined into in the courts of the State, and such expelled member can not maintain a suit in relation to church property nor vote for trustees.(238)

132. *Major Excommunication.*--As excommunication *non tolerati* affects the rights of citizenship, it is not lawful in England nor the United States. To say that A. has been excommunicated in any form, if untrue, is slander.(239)

133. *Vote, Sentence.*--When a vote of excommunication from a church has been passed in the Congregational church and the offender thereby declared no longer a member, the sentence may be promulgated by being read in the presence of the congregation by the pastor.(240)

134. *Trustees, Disqualified.*--The trustees of a church who have been excommunicated are not thereby disqualified in law to act as trustees.(241)

135. *Devise, Void.*--A parent may leave money to a child payable in yearly installments on condition that said child shall continue to be a member of a particular church and attend the regular meetings thereof, and in case he fail so to do that the bequest be thereupon paid to a missionary society. Such a devise is not contrary to the constitution of the State of Wisconsin and is not void for any other reason.(242)

136. *Fraternity, Excommunicated, Bequest.*--Where a church member was also a member of an insurance fraternity connected with his church, the constitution of which required that every member of the fraternity should be and remain a practical Roman Catholic, when he was excommunicated from membership in the church he thereby forfeited his benefit certificate in such fraternity.(243) Also, a condition that a bequest shall be forfeited if the legatee should not marry a Protestant wife, the daughter of Protestant parents who have always been Protestants, was held to be valid and not an infringement of any constitutional right.(244)

137. *Action, Expulsion.*--An action can not be maintained against the parish corporation for expulsion from the church.(245)

138. *Forfeiture of Membership.*--Any member may forfeit his membership in a church.(246)

139. *Insubordination, Expulsion, Hearing.*--The authorities in the church, under its rules and discipline, have a right to exclude members in the church, for insubordination.(247) If the church has no rules as to expulsion of members, the common law prevails, and a member can not be expelled without due notice and fair hearing.(248)

140. *Injunction, Mandamus, Sepulture.*--An injunction will not be granted to prevent the expulsion of a member contrary to the charter and by-laws of the denomination; but if a member be expelled without warrant of law, he has his remedy by mandamus for reinstatement.(249) A person who has been expelled can not maintain an action for restoration in order to enjoy the right of sepulture, as it is premature.(250)

141. *Expulsion, Illegal.*--The attempt of a minority of a church to expel the majority of the members and turn over the property to another denomination is illegal. However, the same would be true if it were done by the majority.(251)

142. *Freedom, Faith, Doctrine.*--The constitution in declaring the freedom of all men to worship God according to the dictates of their own consciences, does not give a church member the right to repudiate the faith and doctrine on which the church was founded, and at the same time to insist on his right to exercise and enjoy the benefits and privileges of a member of such church.(252) Every person joining a church, impliedly, if not expressly, agrees to conform to its rules and to submit to its authority and discipline.(253) A person who has been expelled from a religious society can not maintain an action for services rendered the society while he was a member.(254)

CHAPTER XII.

ELECTIONS

143. *Time, Place, Void.*--Where a religious society that is incorporated holds an election for trustees, which is held at the wrong time or place, the election is void.(255)

144. *Voting, Communicants, Attendance.*--A by-law of a church that prohibited any person whose pew rent was in arrears more than two years from voting at a church meeting, is valid and reasonable.(256) Where a charter of a religious society allowed only members being communicants to vote after they had attained the age of eighteen years, to entitle a member of the congregation to vote it was necessary that he should have taken the sacraments after the age of eighteen years.(257) Where the right to vote was limited to members who contributed not less than ten shillings annually toward the support of the church, those who were challenged for want of complying with the rule can not do so after being challenged and then vote.(258) Stated attendance at divine worship in the church, congregation, or society, and contribution to the support of such church, may be made the tests of the right of a person to be a voter at an election. The attendance of a wife or children of the family is not sufficient to confer the right to vote on the husband or father.(259)

145. *Voters, Poll List.*--Parol evidence is admissible to prove the number of persons entitled to vote in a church society, notwithstanding that there is a register of names of the stated hearers in such church kept by the clerk of the trustees.

146. *Notice, Quorum, Majority, Strangers.*--It is not necessary that a majority of the members of a religious society be present to constitute a corporate meeting. Those present at a regularly called meeting of which due notice has been given to all the members, constitute a quorum; and, in the absence of a rule to the contrary, a majority of the votes cast carries any question.(260) The presence of strangers, unless they vote, will not vitiate the proceedings. If they should vote, unless their votes determine the election, it will not be void.(261) The casting of a few illegal votes that would not change the result of the election does not make it void.(262)

147. *Challenge, Ground.*--The right of a person to vote at any meeting may be challenged. The proper time to challenge a voter is when he offers his vote. After his vote has been received it can not be thrown out on the ground that he was disqualified.(263) A church election for which due notice has been given, that has been fairly conducted, and all the requirements of the statute or rules of the church complied with, is conclusive.(264) Without due notice, all proceedings are void.(265)

148. *By-Laws, Usage.*--If there is no law of a religious society determining the mode of conducting an election, the corporation may provide by-laws therefor; and if the corporation should fail to make such by-laws, a long established usage will govern.(266) Also, if the time an election is to be held is provided for, but the manner of conducting it is not, the meeting may be conducted according to established usage.(267)

149. *Ballot, Hand Vote.*--The vote of a religious society at an annual meeting for the election of officers that the officers shall always be chosen by ballot, does not vitiate an election of officers by hand vote at a subsequent annual meeting. But a provision in the constitution or by-laws requiring a ballot must be complied with.(268)

150. *Hold Over, Successors.*--When the election of the new trustees is invalid, the old trustees hold over until there will have been a valid election of their successors.(269) But where a board that was illegally elected employed a minister who had no notice of such illegality, he was entitled to his compensation according to the contract.(270)

151. *Majority, Votes Cast.*--Where the majority of a congregation protested against the proposed candidate, but failed to vote for any one, such candidate who received the greatest number of votes cast, was lawfully elected.(271)

152. *By-Law, Tickets.*--When a by-law provides that "if besides the names there are other things upon the tickets, such tickets are not to be counted," a ballot having an engraved eagle on it should be rejected.(272) However, in a very recent case under a statute that specifically provided what should be printed on the general election ballot, and in addition thereto the Union Labor label was printed thereon, the court held that the statute should be strictly construed in favor of the voter and that the ticket should be counted.(273)

CHAPTER XIII.

OFFICERS

153. *Charter, By-Laws.*--The articles of organization or the charter which is the constitution of the corporation may provide who may be officers of a religious society and limit their authority. The constitution usually gives further authority to make by-laws which are binding on the officers as well as on the members.(274)

154. *Unincorporated Church, Incorporated.*--The officers of an unincorporated church can only be elected by the members of the church, unless there is some law of the State or rule of the church that provides for appointing them. In an incorporated congregation, the charter and by-laws of the corporation determine whether the officers shall be elected or appointed.(275)

155. *Trustees, Control.*--A statute passed in 1813 providing that a certificate of incorporation by the bishop, vicar-general, pastor of the church, and two others selected by them and their successors shall be a body corporate, does not constitute the trustees the corporation in place of the congregation so as to make the acts of a majority of the trustees binding on the corporation in the absence of proof of other authority.(276) Under the statutes of Louisiana providing for the incorporation of congregations for the purpose of administration and revenues, it was held that the corporation had full control and was responsible to the congregation alone and could not be controlled by the clergy. The congregation had the right to elect others in the places of those removed by reason of their misuse or abuse of their powers.(277) And in Massachusetts, under the law for incorporating Catholic parishes, no one but the trustees have any power.(278)

156. *Membership, Office.*--Where church membership is necessary to hold office in the church corporation, it is a binding condition precedent.(279) An officer who withdraws or is expelled from a religious organization thereby terminates his office.(280)

157. *Certificate of Election.*--A certificate of election of officers is prima facia evidence thereof, but the truth may be shown *aliunde* and a wrong certificate may be canceled by a judgment of a competent court on a writ of *quo warranto* or proceeding under a statute of the State. Also, if the certificate does not conform to the law, it is insufficient.(281)

158. *Term, Successors, Contest.*--Where there is no term of office fixed, the presumption is that an officer continues as such until proof to the contrary is established,(282) or until his successor shall have been elected and shall have qualified.(283) Also, the officers elected for a certain term can not be removed by electing new officers before the end of the term.(284) When officers or committees have been elected "for the ensuing year," they shall hold office until superseded by their duly elected successors. Where two sets of officers were elected at a meeting of a religious corporation and the set that was elected according to the charter continued in office by appointment thereafter, it was too late for the irregularly elected officers to make a contest for the offices after the term for which they had been elected had expired.(285)

159. *By-Laws, Preside.*--At an election of trustees under by-laws that provide that certain officers shall preside, if there are no such officers members may be selected to preside in their places.(286)

160. *Note, Overdraft, Interest.*--The president and secretary of a church corporation have no authority to make a promissory note unless authorized by the board of trustees.(287) Neither has the treasurer authority to make an overdraft on a bank with the action of the trustees.(288) The trustees of a parish, however, may make a note binding the congregation for the payment of the money used in building a church.(289) But when the trustees have an interest in the transaction, adverse to the congregation, they are disqualified from acting.(290) When trustees had claims against the congregation which they included with other claims that third parties had against the church, they could not put them in a judgment note so as to get a lien upon the church property. When officers do not bind the congregation, they usually bind themselves.(291) The trustees of an unincorporated church can not bind it beyond the expressed powers granted by the members.(292)

161. *Board, Control.*--When the laws of the organization give control of matters to the board of trustees, the majority of the members of the church can not control the action of the trustees contrary to the usages and regulations of the church.(293)

162. *Treasurer, Accepting a Draft.*--A parish treasurer has no authority under any condition to bind the corporation by accepting a draft in favor of a third person. A treasurer elected for the purpose of receiving and investing funds in his individual name, holds such funds as trustee for the church and is subject as such trustee to a court of equity. Persons claiming to be trustees of a church but never getting possession of their offices or the property of the church, can not maintain an action against other persons who are in possession and have been duly elected.(294)

163. *Note, Trustees.*--A church will not be bound by a note which was executed by two of its trustees and sent around to other trustees to sign it, where there was no vote of the board of trustees at an authorized meeting to borrow or to execute such note.(295) A meeting of a board must be called as required by law or the by-laws of the organization, and in the absence of any such all members must be notified a reasonable time before the time fixed for holding the meeting. However, if all the trustees are present and agree to hold a meeting it is valid; but it would be well to put such consent in writing and have all the members sign it. (296)

164. *Money, Powers.*--The treasurer of a congregation has no right to return to members moving out of the parish a part of the money paid for the church by them.(297) Officers of a corporation have no powers only those conferred upon them by the charter and by-laws of the corporation or by a majority vote of a duly called meeting of the congregation.(298) When the trustees of a church are authorized to execute contracts for the church, they should act as a body or delegate the power to one of their number or ratify the acts of one of their number.(299) The individual disjointed action of trustees of a religious society, at various times and places, although assented to by a majority, is not the action of the board, and is not binding on the society. To make the action of the board of trustees binding, they must duly meet and by a vote determine their action.(300)

165. *De Facto Officers.*--The acts of *de facto* officers can not usually be questioned in a collateral proceeding, such as to set aside a conveyance, when the merits of the question do not involve the election.(301) Being elected does not alone make a person a *de facto* officer; but he must also be acting in the particular office to which he claims to have been elected.(302) But one who has entered into a contract with the officers of a congregation is estopped from denying their authority to make such contract.(303)

166. *Trustees, Thanks, Charge.*--Where trustees have taken care of funds without charge, the only entry kept being a vote of thanks from time to time, they could not afterward charge a commission on the moneys handled by them for such services.(304)

167. *Discretion, Excommunication.*--A court has no authority to control the exercise of the judgment or discretion of the officers of a church in the management of its funds so long as they do not violate its constitution or by-laws. (305) Excommunication does not always remove an officer of a church corporation.(306) The legal rights of a bishop in regard to the temporalities of a church where they are not prescribed by civil law, must rest, if at all, upon the ecclesiastical law, which must be determined by evidence.(307)

168. *Key, Possession, Right.*--Having the key of a church, is prima facia evidence of possession, but the right of possession is a matter of proof.(308)

169. *Church, Bishop, Debts, Salary of a Priest.*--Where a church is not itself liable because it is not incorporated, the Roman Catholic bishop of the diocese is not personally liable for moneys borrowed by the pastors of such church in the name of the church, which were partly invested in real estate which was put in the bishop's name in the usual manner, although the bishop's permission was necessary before borrowing the money, and notwithstanding that the bishop raised some of the money to pay some of the debts and the mortgage on the real estate of the church on his personal security, and he received part of the borrowed funds from a dying pastor and handed it over to his successor.(309) Also, a bishop is not personally liable for the salary of a priest whom he engages. They are fellow servants working for the Church and not in the relation of employer and employee any more than are a general and captain in the same army.(310)

170. *Note, Building Committee.*--In an action on a note given by the pastor of a church for money borrowed to pay bills for the erection of the church building, in which the plaintiff sought to charge the building committee, and it appeared from the plaintiff's testimony that the title to the property was in the bishop and the committee did not handle any of the funds, but was a shifting body to whom the pastor only went for advice and consultation, it was held that the plaintiff could not recover.(311)

171. *Fraud, Trust.*--Where a "prophet" induced members of his organization, by his fraud and deceit, to convey to him all their property in discharge of a religious duty and then refused to account to them, the court declared the trust closed and divided the estate among the members in proportion to the money, property, and labor contributed by each of them.(312)

172. *Superioress, Money.*--A person who contributed money for the purpose of repairing a convent, the money being turned over to the superioress and the convent not being incorporated, upon the project being abandoned subsequently a personal judgment could not be obtained against the superioress for the money contributed.(313)

173. *Loan, Priest.*--If a man lends money to a priest for the purpose of paying a note against the congregation left at the bank for collection, he can recover the money so paid from the congregation.(314)

174. *Warden, Wages, Sexton.*--A church warden who was hired by the trustees of a church can not collect his wages by an action against the priest of the parish. (315) A church accepting the services of a sexton is liable to him therefor, whether the by-laws were observed in employing him or not; nor will the fact that any party (as in this case the Ladies of the Altar Society) agreed to contribute to his annual salary, defeat his recovery of the whole from the church employing him.(316)

175. *Sewing Circle, Money.*--A church may maintain an action against a sewing circle to require it to pay over money collected for the benefit of the church.(317)

CHAPTER XIV.

MEETINGS

176. *Business, Notice, Meeting.*--Where, in the transaction of the local business of a religious society, whether incorporated or not, meetings of the members shall become necessary, in order to make such meetings legal due notice thereof should be given to every member. The notice should specify the exact time and place where the meeting will be held, and no change can be made except at such time and place. Unless some other place is specified, the parish church is the proper place for holding meetings. If the church should be locked and the key can not be found, a meeting should be held at the door or at the nearest practical place to the church where all the members may assemble, and then by a majority vote they may adjourn to any convenient near place accessible to all the members.(318)

177. *Acts, Void, Lawful, Clerk.*--The acts of a majority of the members of a corporation, unless done according to law and in conformity with the charter and by-laws of the corporation, are absolutely null and void.(319) The only lawful manner by which a congregation can express itself, is by a meeting regularly called and held upon due notice.(320) The notice of a meeting should be authorized by the trustees or other authority of the church, and given to all the members. The clerk of the board of trustees, unless authorized to do so, has no authority to sign the name of the members of the board to a notice, and a meeting called in that way is illegal.(321)

178. *Special Meeting, Notice.*--When a meeting is special, the notice must state for what purpose the meeting is called. If it fails to do so it is void, and unless all the members are present and consent to the holding of the meeting, all business transacted is illegal and void.(322) Notice of a special meeting that states one specific purpose for which it is called, and then states "to transact any other business that may legally come before the meeting," is not good for any purpose except the one specified.(323)

179. *Meeting, Consent.*--A valid meeting can not be held by a corporation, unless notice has been given in conformity with the laws and rules and regulations of the corporation or the consent of every person who is entitled to be present at the holding of such meeting. In the latter case the consent should be in writing and signed by all the members.(324) However, a person who attends a meeting and takes part in it without objection, is estopped from raising the question of notice.(325)

180. *Notice, Principal Service, Custom.*--When a rule of a church required notice of a meeting to be given at the principal service, a notice given at an earlier service only, was void.(326) But where the ordinances of a church specified that the election of officers should be at least six days before the end of their term, and it became the custom of the church to hold the election on a movable holiday which sometimes was less than six days, the election was held valid.(327)

181. *Adjournment.*--Where a meeting was noticed for one day and held on a different day without notice of adjournment, all acts done were void and the officers elected were neither *de jure* nor *de facto* officers.(328)

182. *Proof of the Notice.*--The proper proof of the notice would be the return of the officer serving the notice, in some States; and in others an affidavit of the person who served the notice. The proof of the services of a summons would be sufficient unless there is some other law or rule to the contrary.(329)

183. *Presiding Officer.*--When the laws of the organization provide who shall preside at a meeting, but the minister contrary to such laws and against objections presided over the majority of the congregation, and the minority was presided over by the proper person, and both elected officers, the officers elected by the minority were the lawful ones.(330) However, where a meeting is presided over without objection by a member instead of the proper officer, the acts of the body are lawful.(331)

184. *Voters, Rules.*--Unless the laws of the State otherwise provide, every religious organization has the right to determine who shall vote at its meetings and elections. If those provisions are reasonable, they are lawful. Under such provisions it has been repeatedly held that where there are rules requiring annual subscriptions to the church,(332) only those who rented and paid for pews, or those who paid a certain annual tax, or those who went to communion, were entitled to vote.(333) And where there was no rule, it was held that one who has not contributed to the church(334) and persons who attended church only occasionally and contributed only when they attended, were not qualified voters.(335) In the last case it was stated that a qualified voter is one who has attended regularly during the year and has contributed to the support of the church.

185. *Quorum, Majority.*--A quorum of a congregation usually consists of those present at a duly called regular meeting, and a majority of those present is sufficient to carry questions, unless by rule or law otherwise provided.(336) But where there is a definite body in a corporation which has established no other rule, a majority of the members of the corporation constitute a quorum.(337) Where the minutes of the clerk stated that upon due notice the members of the corporation met, a quorum is presumed.(338)

186. *Votes, Challenge, Inspectors, Casting Vote.*--The reception of illegal votes does not invalidate an election unless they change the result.(339) If the presiding officer refuses to allow a qualified voter to vote, the right may be enforced through civil courts.(340) When votes have been received without challenge, it is then too late to raise the objection that the persons have no right to vote.(341) It is the duty of the inspectors to determine the qualifications of an elector at the time that he offers to vote, and before he votes; and if they decide in the exercise of their judgment, without malice or improper motives, the regularity of the election can not be questioned.(342) When a rule allows the presiding officer to vote and another rule states that he shall have the casting vote in case of a tie vote, he still had the right to cast the decisive vote.(343) Illegal voting in a religious society probably is not an indictable offense, but it is a disorderly act.(344)

187. *Written Notice, Prayer Meeting.*--Where a five days' written notice is required to hold church meetings, an oral notice given on Sunday evening at the prayer meeting is not sufficient for a meeting on the following Wednesday. But a vote taken on Sunday to hire the minister and fix his salary, is not void.(345) Churches and benefit societies, such as insurance fraternities, being charitable organizations, may do business concerning such association on Sunday.(346)

188. *Expulsion, Damages.*--A man who has been wrongfully expelled from a temperance society for religious reasons may recover damages therefor.(347)

CHAPTER XV.

CHURCH RECORDS

189. *Evidence, Entries, Minutes.*--The record of the proceedings of a religious society is evidence as to its doings, both in its own tribunals and the courts of the State. Such record consists of entries required to be made by the laws or rules of the society, the laws of the State, and the minutes adopted by the society. Therefore, it is of the greatest importance that it be kept with great exactness, omitting nothing that is important.(348) Also, the minutes of all the meetings should be correct before being duly adopted. All erasures and interlineations should be certified by the clerk and then signed by him.

190. *Uniformity.*--Every entry required to be kept by the laws of the State as well as the rules of the Church, should be kept as to births, marriages, and death. Every diocese should have uniform record books in all parishes and every pastor should keep blanks printed in the form of a page of the record book, to issue certificates when required.

191. *Marriage, Death, Baptism, Birth, Church Records.*--The church records duly kept in accordance with the discipline of the church, are admissible in evidence to prove marriage, death, and baptism. Where the record is incomplete, as giving the date of baptism only, it is not admissible in proof of date of birth. But if it gives the date of birth, it is prima facia proof thereof.(349)

192. *Certified Copies.*--Under statutes, certified copies of the record made by the custodian thereof are admissible in evidence in any case where the original would be admissible. Also, one who had compared a copy with the original record may testify to the same. The rule, as given, substantially prevails under statutes in the following States: Alabama, Georgia, Illinois, Indiana, Kansas, Kentucky, Louisiana, Maryland, Minnesota, Missouri, Oklahoma, Pennsylvania, Rhode Island, and Wisconsin; and also, in Ontario, Manitoba, and the Dominion of Canada.

193. *Rule of Admissibility.*--A certified copy of the record of a baptism taken from a church register by the parish priest, when admissible at the place where such record is kept, as in Ireland, is admissible to prove the same fact in the State of Missouri.(350)

194. *Proper Record.*--A book kept by a minister, which contained a regular statement in proper form of the admission of members, choice of officers, and transaction of business of the church, which was the only book kept by the parish, is the proper record of the church.(351)

195. *Name, Record.*--The author would like to emphasize the importance of correct records. Frequently we find no Christian name given in the records of birth, which practically makes the record worthless. When a child is born it is entitled to a name, immediately, which should be given and be correct. At least the first Christian name should be correct; a mistake in a middle name is not material. This is true of deeds and records of all kinds, but practically of births, deaths, and marriages.(352)

CHAPTER XVI.

CHURCH TRIBUNALS

196. *Jurisdiction, Privileges.*--It is usual for every fraternity to have a tribunal of its own for the trial of members who break its laws or violate its discipline. Within their jurisdiction, the laws of the State give such tribunals great privileges and courts show them great respect. The Freemasons, the Knights of Columbus, etc., and most of the churches, have such courts.(353)

197. *Trial, Property, Priest.*--In most of the States a court will not interfere with the fair trial of a church tribunal. Neither will the court entertain a controversy concerning the title or right of possession of real or personal property excepting at the instance of some person claiming a right thereto derived from or recognized by the law of the State or of the United States.(354) But when the bishop has deprived a subordinate priest of his authority to officiate as such, he may enjoin the priest from making use of the church property.(355)

198. *Doubt, Legal Rights.*--The foregoing rule has some doubt cast on it in Delaware and Massachusetts. The investigation of a dispute between members of a church by a committee according to church regulations, consented to by the parties, in which both take part, can have no effect on their legal rights. If the State law provides for cases of the kind, it is superior and must be submitted to. Also, an award or proceeding of a committee is not evidence for or against either party. However, any statement made, or admissions of the parties, if not of a recognized confidential nature, may be given in evidence on the trial in a court of the State.(356) The judgment of a mutual ecclesiastical council legally convoked will not bind either party rejecting it.(357)

199. *Bishop, Priest, Redress.*--When a bishop removes a priest in the regular way according to the rules and discipline of his church, the priest has no redress. (358) Also, when a priest has submitted his case to the church tribunal according to the discipline of his church, he must abide by its decision, excepting where his civil rights or property rights as a citizen are involved, when he may appeal to the laws of the land.(359)

200. *Trial, Counsel.*--The question whether a minister on trial in a church tribunal is entitled to be heard by counsel or attorneys depends upon the laws of the church, and it can not be said as a matter of law that he is entitled to counsel. (360)

201. *Removal, Suspension, Trial.*--In the United States under the laws and discipline of the Catholic Church a priest may be removed from the charge of a congregation at the pleasure of the bishop, without trial; but he can not be suspended from his priestly functions without specific accusation and trial.(361)

202. *Charges, Fair Trial, Hearsay Evidence.*--When a clergyman or officer is to be removed or a member of the congregation is to be excommunicated, it is necessary to fully state the charges against him and give him an opportunity for a fair trial according to the laws and rules of the religious society before rendering final judgment. All the allegations of the complaint should be made upon positive knowledge of the complainant or upon evidence that is admissible to prove the case in court. Rumor or gossip, known as mere hearsay evidence, is not sufficient to base a charge against the character of any one.(362)

203. *Trial, Testimony, Slander.*--A church judgment, where there has been a full and fair trial or when members submit to the church tribunal, and the judgment has only been rebuke, censure, suspension, or excommunication, is usually upheld by the courts; and when the testimony given on such trial is concerning immoral or scandalous conduct or crime, if those taking part act in good faith and within the scope of the authority of the church, they are protected by law and not liable to an action for damages for libel or slander.(363)

204. *Remedies, Secular Courts.*--In cases involving church doctrine and discipline only, all remedies within the church must be exhausted by a member before the secular courts will interfere, if they will interfere at all.(364)

205. *Notice, Waiver.*--When the laws of the church provide the tribunal and procedure, if the person proceeded against avoids the service of the notice or refuses to submit to the court, the notice of trial required to be served might thereby be considered waived and the tribunal might proceed with the trial in the absence of the accused.(365)

206. *Appeal, Decision, Limitation.*--The right to appeal from one court to another of higher jurisdiction is generally recognized.(366) If after trial in the lower tribunal of the Church, an appeal is taken, the decision on the appeal is binding upon the parties and also upon the inferior tribunal.(367) In the Anglican and some other churches, there is no limitation as to time when offenses against the discipline of the church may be inquired into.(368)
The Catholic Church has a limitation as to prescriptive rights, to-wit: "Three years in case of movable property; ten years in case of a right, or of immovable property, *inter praesentes*; twenty years in the same case, *inter absentes*."(369) Also, there are limitations in canonical cases, varying from one to twenty years. (370) There is no statute of limitation on lawful debts.

207. *Procedure, Judge, Juror, Witness.*--If there are no rules of procedure prescribed by the church tribunal, the proper practice is to follow the State courts; as, for example, where the State law forbids an officer of the court who has an interest in the proceeding to sit as judge or juror, the same would apply to the church tribunal, it being the common law of the land. Also, in States where a person who is interested in a matter is not a competent witness, in the absence of a different rule in the church, the same rule would apply in the church tribunal. (371)

208. *Catholic Discipline.*--A church member has no right to sue any one in holy orders in the civil court without leave. That is, a layman or priest should obtain leave of the bishop to sue a priest. In some countries it is ground for excommunication to violate the rule. This rule is analogous to the general rule that a sovereign state can not be sued without its consent.(372) In this country, where there is no ecclesiastical court recognized in law, leave is rarely asked.(373)

CHAPTER XVII.

STATE COURTS

209. *Decision, Ecclesiastical Matter.*--The decision of the highest tribunal of the church on a purely ecclesiastical matter will not be disturbed by civil courts unless it is in open defiance and express violation of the constitution of such body.(374)

210. *Right of Property, Civil Rights.*--Where there are several church tribunals one above another, when the highest tribunal having jurisdiction of the case has decided a question as to the right of property, a civil court will accept such decision of the church tribunal as conclusive.(375) The courts give way to the usages and regulations of the church so far as they are not inconsistent with the constitution and laws of the State.(376) As far as civil rights are concerned, the statute of limitations may be pleaded even where those rights are founded upon some law or rule of the denomination.(377)

211. *Creed, Factions, Property, Management.*--The supreme court exercises no ecclesiastical jurisdiction, but accepts what the highest ecclesiastical authority in each church promulgates as the faith and practice of that church, and will not determine for itself what that faith or creed is in order to establish the rights of respective factions in the church to the church property. But a majority of a congregation that secedes from the church and forms a new organization can not claim any of the property.(378) The civil courts will not interfere with church management so far as concerns the spiritual discipline of the members, but where civil rights of property are involved, the courts may determine them.(379) The civil rights of a religious society or its members are within the jurisdiction of the State courts.(380)

212. *Trust, Court of Equity.*--A conveyance in trust for the use of a church vests the use in the church and it will be protected by a court of equity.(381)

213. *Injunction, Closing Church, Paying Money, Disturbances.*--A court of equity will issue an injunction against the trustees of a church from wrongfully closing it or keeping it closed even against a small minority.(382) Church property vested in trustees of a religious body is held under trust and a court of equity has jurisdiction to enforce the trust.(383) A court of equity may restrain the trustees of a church from paying money to a duly deposed minister.(384) But a court of equity will not interfere to quell religious disturbances when no question as to property or civil rights is involved. The board of trustees of a church can not remove a priest against the will of the congregation.(385)

214. *Suits, Parties.*--Where a number of persons have contributed to the erection of a church, it is not necessary for all who contribute to join in an action to restrain a sale of the property for mercantile purposes.(386) Any member of a church not incorporated may come into a court of equity in behalf of himself and others and enforce the execution of a trust in favor of the church.(387) The same rule would apply to a church where any one in authority is violating the law.(388) If several congregations of a diocese are interested in litigation, to hold all the property of the diocese liable for the debt of a parish, each congregation is entitled to be made a party.(389)

215. *Complaint.*--A complaint that the plaintiffs hold one doctrinal standard and the defendants another is sufficiently definite without explaining the difference between the two.(390)

216. *Church Tribunal, Courts.*--Courts are reluctant to interfere in the church doctrine or discipline or inquire into the regularity of the proceedings of the church tribunal. When such tribunal has deposed a pastor or expelled a member, it is final. However, in contracts, property rights, and civil rights of a citizen, the courts take jurisdiction. It is no defense to a pastor's expulsion that there is salary due him.(391)

217. *Unincorporated Congregation, Actions, Interest.*--An unincorporated congregation may be sued on contract in its associate capacity, though no persons are named as trustees or committeeman.(392) In all actions by or against a congregation the civil courts will not permit suits to be brought by complainants who have no interest either legal or equitable in the temporalities of the church.(393) A suit against a society of Shakers consisting of indefinite membership with changing additions, withdrawals, and deaths, whose property is held in common without any individual interest, may properly be brought in equity as the remedy at law would be inadequate.(394)

218. *Blasphemy, Sabbath, Lord's Prayer, Bible.*--Christianity is a part of the common law of the United States; it is on this ground that blasphemy and violation of the Sabbath are made criminal offenses and that the Lord's Prayer and the Bible are used in the schools.(395)

CHAPTER XVIII.

EVIDENCE

219. *Judicial Notice.*--A church takes judicial notice without proof of its own rules, laws, and doctrines. Every other fact should be proved according to the rules of evidence of the church, and in the absence of a church rule the following rules of the courts of this country should prevail:

1. Nothing should be admitted in evidence unless it directly proves or disproves an evidentiary fact forming a link of a chain of facts that will prove a fact in issue.
2. It is sufficient to prove the substance of the issue, unless the exact word or thing forms the issue.
3. The burden of proof is on the one who asserts the fact, whether it is stated affirmatively or negatively, and its proof is necessary to his making a case.
4. The best evidence that the case in its nature affords must be produced.
5. Mere hearsay evidence shall not be allowed, excepting:
    (a) Matters of public or general interest.
    (b) Declaration against interest.
    (c) Dying declarations.
    (d) The testimony of witnesses since dead or absent.
    (e) Admissions.
    (f) Confessions.

220. *Competent Witness.*--Everybody who has the use of reason and understands the import of an oath is a competent witness.

221. *Confessions, Secret Societies.*--At common law, confessions were admissible; but there is no case in the United States since 1813 where the court has sent a priest to jail for contempt for refusing to disclose a confession, and no case in which a priest disclosed a confession. Immediately after a priest was committed for contempt for refusing to divulge the secrets of the confessional, in 1813, New York enacted the following law: "No minister of the gospel, or priest of any denomination whatsoever, shall be allowed to disclose any confession made to him in his professional character, in the course of discipline enjoined by the rules or practice of such denomination." A similar law has been adopted in the following States and Territories: Alabama, Arizona, California, Colorado, Idaho, Iowa, Kansas, Kentucky, Michigan, Missouri, Nebraska, Nevada, North Dakota, Ohio, New York, Oklahoma, South Dakota, Utah, Washington, Wisconsin, Wyoming, and Hawaii. The secrets of a secret society are not privileged, and a member as a witness must answer all relevant questions in court.(396)

222. *Privilege, Answer.*--When a question concerning a matter privileged is put, the priest should say: "I claim my privilege as a clergyman and ask the court not to require me to answer"; "Whatever he said concerning the matter, was said to me in the confessional as a priest"; "I talked with him about the matter only in my professional capacity as a priest and confessor"; "I did not speak to him about the matter except in my confidential capacity as priest;" or a similar statement that sets up the clergyman's privilege without giving facts. A clergyman should not say: "He confessed it to me," or "He told it to me in confession," or give any other answer that implies what was said in confession, as jurors are always watching for a hint of what was said. Neither should the priest say, "I refuse to answer," without stating that he refuses because of his privilege as a clergyman. The trial judge or the attorneys trying the case may put proper questions to determine whether the information was given the witness in the confessional or in his capacity as confessor.(397)

223. *Admissions, False Statements.*--Admissions or statements made to a clergyman not in his capacity of confidential adviser or in the course of discipline, are not privileged.(398) Neither are false statements made to a committee investigating charges; but all statements made to such a committee or an officer of the church, unless false and made with malice, are privileged.(399)

224. *Anonymous Letter, Clergyman.*--Where a priest received an anonymous letter alleged to have been written by a defendant, which he read to her, he was not disqualified from testifying that she was excited and that she stated she had no idea how the fire started, and that the letter was unknown to her, etc.(400) The mere fact that a communication is made to a clergyman does not make it privileged. It is privileged only when made in confidence of the relation and under such circumstances as to imply that it should forever remain a secret in the breast of the confidential adviser.(401) When a matter is privileged, it is not left to the witness whether or not he shall testify concerning it; but he can not testify without the consent of the other party.(402)

225. *Voire Dire.*--Where a priest made a preliminary examination of a woman to ascertain her mental capacity to make a confession, her answers in such preliminary examination were admissible in a contest on a will; but her confession was not admissible.(403)

226. *England, Confession.*--The rule is now accorded priests in England, but was not formerly. Where a priest turned a watch over to its owner, the court ordered him, under pain of contempt, to tell where he got the watch.(404) But in another case it was held that a priest need not divulge the confession of a defendant who was held for crime.(405)

227. *United States, Rules.*--In the United States courts, the rule prevails that such confidential communications to a priest shall not be divulged.(406)

228. *Presumptions, Usage.*--The usage of a church or the laws of its organization as a religious society, if they are to be considered in deciding legal controversies, must be proved as facts.(407) In the absence of proof, it will be presumed that subordinate bodies, as congregations, can not dissolve their connection with the principal organization without permission.(408)

229. *Funeral Expenses.*--Witnesses' opinions as to the reasonable amount for burial or as to the cost of a funeral being reasonable, are not binding on a court or jury. The station of a man, the property that he leaves, the life that he has followed, all should be considered by the court. The whims and notions of societies and others are of minor consideration. Those who make funeral expenses that are not allowed by the court must pay them.(409)

CHAPTER XIX.

CONTRACTS

230. *Business, Religious Service.*--A church organization has the legal right to make any contract concerning its own affairs that is not prohibited by its by-laws or its charter, subject to all laws of legal contracts in the business world. When the consideration is a religious service duly performed, there seems to be no objection to it. Therefore, a minister may collect for preaching a sermon, attending the sick, or saying prayers, or performing any other religious service. But an incorporated church has no authority to enter into a contract for an ulterior purpose, such as the employment of a vessel for the purpose of an excursion. (410)

231. *Incorporated Body.*--The only way a religious society that is incorporated can make a contract is by a vote of the aggregate body or of the board of trustees, or through an agent authorized by a vote of one body or the other.(411)

232. *Mortgage, Deficiency Judgment.*--Where a mortgage had been foreclosed against church property before the congregation was incorporated, a deficiency judgment can not be rendered against such church corporation.(412) But where a congregation was incorporated after a debt had been incurred and took charge of the property, it assumed the debt.(413)

233. *Building Contracts.*--The taking part in a meeting by voting and appointing committees to make contracts will bind those taking part in all contracts made in accordance with the directions of such meeting. In some States the individuals are held only to the amount that each subscribes, but in other States each individual is liable for the entire debt.(414)

234. *Individual Promise, Subscriptions, Signature.*--An individual promise to give a donation to charity, can not be enforced.(415) But subscriptions to build a church or other charitable institution or to pay the salary of a clergyman when signed by more than one person, have been held binding in some cases on the disputed rule of a-promise-for-a-promise consideration.(416) In the foregoing cases the donor might revoke his subscription or in case of his death his estate would not be liable.(417) However, when expenses have been made or steps taken in the carrying out of the object of the subscriptions, the general rule is that the subscriptions become binding contracts.(418) If the object of the subscriptions be abandoned or changed without the consent of the subscriber, he is thereby released. A promissory note given for the subscription, unless negotiated for value in due course of trade, does not change the foregoing rules. (419) Where many persons subscribed to build a church and some of them failed to pay, one who paid brought an action on behalf of himself and others and collected the unpaid subscriptions.(420) The defendant Nalty signed "Nalty Family, $1,000," but he was held personally liable.(421)

235. *Special Purpose, Suit.*--When money is subscribed for a special purpose, as for rebuilding a church, it belongs to the church organization; and in a suit to recover the money the action should be brought in the name of the corporation, if incorporated, and if not incorporated it should be brought in the name of the interested party.(422)

236. *Promise, Consideration.*--A promise made by the owner of land to a trustee for the benefit of a religious society, that he would convey the land to such society if it would build a church thereon, is a good and lawful consideration; and after work was begun on the church, the contract was enforceable in a court of equity.(423)

CHAPTER XX.

PEWS

237. *Sold, Rented.*--Prior to the Reformation pews were not sold nor rented and every member had the right to sit wherever he pleased in the body of the church. After the Reformation, the ordinary or bishop was granted the right of "faculty" to rent or sell pews.(424)

238. *Incorporeal Hereditament.*--The English title in a pew is in the nature of a right of way through another's land; it is an incorporeal hereditament. In the absence of express law, the title to pews in this country is said to be in the nature of real estate, and in fact not very different from the English title.(425) In some States the title is made personal property by statute.(426) And in others the courts have inquired into the law of the church and adjudged the title accordingly. (427) The general rule is that the owner of a pew simply has an easement.(428)

239. *Catholic Church, Pew Rights.*--In the Catholic Church, by the canon law, the ownership in or control over a pew is forbidden to laymen. Notwithstanding that, if the party holding the title violates the rule of the church by giving a deed to the pew-holder, the courts would probably sustain his title.(429) However, as the clergy can neither rent nor sell pews without becoming subject to the law of the land and the jurisdiction of our courts, it is important to know what the law of the State is.

240. *Land, Use, Rent Pews.*--Where land was conveyed in trust to the bishop of a diocese and his successors for the erection of a church for the use of a congregation, the right to rent pews vested under the deed and laws of the Catholic Church in the parish priest and not in the trustees afterward elected, as the parish priest was the agent of the bishop.(430)

241. *Trustees, Sale in Perpetuity.*--Without authority of law the trustees of a church can not make an absolute sale in perpetuity of a pew without any reservation of rent.(431) The sale of a pew in a church will be determined in a case according to the particular facts.(432)

242. *Pew, Right to Occupy, Conditions.*--A grant of a church pew in perpetuity does not give the owner an absolute right of property as a grant of land in fee; but gives only a right to sit therein, although he may maintain an action in court for protection of his rights.(433) In Vermont a pew holder has only the right to occupy his seat during religious services and holds it subject to the superior right of the society owning the pew.(434) A condition in the deed to a pew that a holder about to leave the congregation shall offer it to the society for a certain price, is not invalid.(435) Where a pew holder held his pew by a certain agreement and after the church had been remodeled he bought a different pew, the conditions attached to the first pew did not apply to the last.(436) Pews owned by the occupant pass to the heirs as real estate instead of going to the executors as personal property in States where the title is in the nature of the title to real estate.(437)

243. *Tax, Assessment.*--A tax assessed upon the pew of a religious corporation in part for purposes not specifically named in a deed of the pew, which alone gives the power to make such an assessment and which strictly defines and limits such power, is invalid *in toto*.(438) The right to make an assessment on pews must be founded upon law, else it can not be enforced.(439) When a congregation sells pews at auction rent free for the purpose of building a church, it has no power thereafter to assess the pews for the salary of the minister.(440)

244. *Pew holders' Rights.*--A pew holder has the exclusive right to occupy his pew when the house is used for the purpose for which it was erected; but he can not convert his pew to other purposes not contemplated.(441) If he has paid his pew-rent according to agreement, he is entitled to use his pew on all occasions when the house is occupied, even when it is open for purposes different from those mentioned in the conveyance thereof; and he has the right to exclude all others from his pew by fastening the door or otherwise, and any one who enters his pew knowing the facts, is a trespasser and liable to an action for damages. (442) The owner of a pew has no right to put an offensive covering thereon nor use his pew in any way to the annoyance of the congregation or not in keeping with the place and conditions. By placing anything offensive about his pew, he may be liable for maintaining a nuisance, and such offensive thing may be removed; but, as far as possible, it must be removed without damaging the pew holder's property.(443)

245. *Rebuilding, Remodeling.*--An injunction was granted on the bill of pew holders, restraining the authorities of the church from pulling it down, as they were going to use the materials in the erection of a new church on a different site. On the answer, the injunction was dissolved on the ground that if the complainants had rights which would be violated, there was a remedy at law and that the nature and extent of the injury were not such as called for the interposition of a court of equity by injunction.(444) Where a parish abandons an old church and builds a new one it does not become liable to any pew holder for damages by reason thereof unless it has acted wantonly or intentionally to injure the pew holder.(445) But when it becomes necessary for the purpose of repairing or remodeling a church, to destroy old pews, a pew built by a member under contract with the church can not be removed or destroyed without compensation. (446) Pew rights are subject to the right of the parish to pull down and rebuild a church either as a matter of necessity or expediency, but in the latter case the owner of a pew is entitled to payment.(447) A pew holder has only the right to occupy his pew during public worship, and when the church has become so out of repair that it can not be used for public worship, the owner of a pew can recover only nominal damages for injuries to his pew.(448)

246. *Selling Pew on Execution.*--In an action to recover the value of a pew sold at auction, the merits of the case will be tried according to the law of the land. (449) It is doubtful whether a pew in a church can be sold for private debts of the pew holder.(450) It depends somewhat upon the title and State law of exemptions.(451) To render an attachment of a pew valid, it is not necessary for the officer to come in sight of the pew or even to enter the church.(452)

247. *Members, Pew.*--Members of the congregation may be required to pay for a pew or sitting in the church, and where a priest ejected a member from the church because he would not rent a pew, he was sustained by the court.(453)

248. *Free Church, Seats, Lease.*--The trustees of a free church may assign seats and forcibly remove one from a seat without authority.(454) Where a pew is real estate, a pew holder may acquire the right to it by prescription in the usual way.(455) Where pews are not rented and the members support the church by voluntary subscriptions, they have equal right to the occupancy of the pews. But where the church builds the pews and rents them, a man paying rent for a pew holds it under lease in the nature of a lease to real estate. However, he does not obtain all the rights of a lessee of land, and in many cases a rule of the church governs the holding of pews, which will be observed by the State courts.(456)

249. *Executors, Pew-Rent.*--The executors of a pew owner are not bound to pay pew-rent accrued after the owner's death.
250. *Voting, Pew-Rent, Arrears.*--Where a church is incorporated and by its charter or the laws of the State it has authority to make reasonable by-laws, a bylaw which prohibits any person from voting whose pew-rent is in arrears for more than two years, is valid.(457)

CHAPTER XXI.

PROPERTY

251. *Unincorporated, Trustee.*--The question whether an unincorporated religious society may take a gift or devise, is determined by the law of domicile. (458) Generally an unincorporated religious association can not hold property in its assumed name, but it must be held by conveyance in trust to a trustee named. (459)

252. *Charter, By-Laws.*--When the charter or by-laws of a church corporation provide that they may be altered, such changes may, after the execution and delivery of a deed, immediately adhere to the title.(460)

253. *Suits, Corporation, Members.*--Cases may occur in which the corporation in its corporate capacity, or the society in its collective capacity, may be a plaintiff or a defendant in a suit between it and one or more members of the religious society in their individual capacity or in their collective capacity, in a quasi conspiracy or concerning other torturous acts, or a collective contract.(461)

254. *Deed, Court, Title.*--A deed made in pursuance of an order of a court having jurisdiction passes good title.(462)

255. *Subscription, Lots.*--Any one may convey title to a church as his part of the subscription by merely marking it on a plat made by him, as lots donated to such church.(463)

256. *Misnomer, Identity.*--The misnomer of a religious society or corporation will not invalidate a mortgage where the identity of the society can be clearly shown. (464)

257. *Adverse Possession, Color of Title.*--A religious corporation may obtain title to land by adverse possession. The length of such possession is determined by the laws of the State, the usual period being twenty years.(465) Unless the laws of the State require it, color of title at the time of asserting adverse possession need not be shown.(466)

258. *Sale, Restrictions.*--In some States when not restricted by the laws of the organization the parish corporation may sell the premises in order to pay the church debts. However, it is not a common law right.(467)

259. *Deed.*--A deed to "The Evangelical Order of Christians" was sufficiently definite for a valid conveyance.(468)

260. *Error.*--A clerical error in the name of the grantee will not make a deed void. However, when such error has been discovered, it should be corrected. (469)

261. *Mortgage, Bishop, Debts.*--The archbishop of a church to which property is bequeathed, can not mortgage it without authority from the church or under the law.(470) Also, the bishop of a diocese to whom land had been conveyed in trust for a particular congregation, could not execute a valid mortgage thereon to secure his own indebtedness.(471) But a religious society in the absence of prohibitionary legislation, has power to mortgage its property to secure its debts. (472)

262. *Deed, Trust, Fee.*--A deed of land to a Catholic bishop and his heirs and assigns forever in trust for a Catholic parish for the purpose of a free burial ground, gave the bishop an estate in fee.(473)

263. *Debts, Creditors.*--A committee of a religious society authorized to sell lands to raise money to pay its general debts, is not authorized to execute a mortgage for the purpose of securing various creditors holding claims; and the defect in such mortgage is not cured by a vote at a subsequent meeting to which the committee made a report of its action.(474)

264. *Mortgage or Sale, Notice, Consent.*--Whenever there is to be a mortgage or sale of the church property, if it is to be done by the corporation, it must be done strictly in accordance with the charter and laws of the corporation, and if those do not provide therefor, every member should receive a reasonable notice to attend a meeting of the congregation and the question should be submitted to such meeting and a vote taken thereon. If all the proceedings are regular and the proper officers (president and secretary) of the corporation be authorized to make a conveyance, it is good in law.(475) However, if the irregular acts of officers or members of a congregation are subsequently ratified in a lawful manner, they become binding.(476) When consent of the court is required, it must be obtained.(477)

265. *Title, Taxes, Judicial Notice.*--If the title is in the bishop in fee in accordance with church law it is not "owned by any religious association" and is liable for taxes. The laws of the Catholic Church are not the subject of judicial notice, but must be alleged and proved as any other fact.(478)

266. *Title, Diocese, Rule.*--Where the title to the property of the diocese was in the bishop for the use of the church and subsequently the diocese was incorporated, the bishop was not divested of title and it was still necessary to have the property conveyed by deed.(479) In some other States, however, the contrary rule prevails.(480)

267. *Priest, Deed, Funds.*--Where it was claimed that a priest purchased lands and took the deed in his own name and paid therefor with funds belonging to the congregation, the conveyance will not be decreed by the court only upon the clearest and most satisfactory evidence.(481)

268. *Monks, Missions, Title.*--The fact that the monks or priests were at the head of the missions in California when it was acquired by the United States, does not prove that the Catholic Church had universal ownership of the property.(482) The acts of Congress giving the city of San Antonio authority to sell public lands, was intended, no doubt, to dispose of mission property, but it was held not to affect the Catholic Church, the title to which had been confirmed by another act of Congress.(483)

269. *Texan Revolution, Land.*--At the time of the Texan Revolution, a Catholic church held no real estate of perfect title, but enjoyed only the use of the land that it possessed and continued so to occupy after the admission of Texas into the Union.(484)

270. *Priest, Agent, Deed.*--The priest in charge of a congregation is the agent of the archbishop, and where the title to the real estate is conveyed by absolute deed to the bishop, the congregation, against the protest of the priest and without obtaining leave from the bishop, has no right to tear down a church for the purpose of rebuilding or repairing it.(485) And a priest in charge of mission property may maintain in his name an action to recover its possession.(486)

271. *Devise, Uncertainty.*--A devise of property "to the Roman Catholic Orphans" of a certain diocese, making the bishop of the diocese executor of the will and giving him power to sell the property and use the proceeds for the benefit of the Roman Catholic orphans, is void for uncertainty.(487)

272. *Donor, Ambiguous Provision.*--The religious convictions of the donor may be shown for the purpose of construing an ambiguous provision of a deed or will. (488)

273. *Trust, Evidence.*--Without any trust being declared in writing, parol evidence can not be allowed to prove that the Catholic Church and parsonage is held in trust for the congregation by the bishop of the diocese, notwithstanding that the moneys for purchasing the lands and putting up such buildings were collected by subscriptions and contributions made to the priest in charge under the law, usage, and polity of the Roman Catholic Church.(489) At common law land may be granted to pious uses before there is a grantee to take it. In the meantime, the title is in abeyance.(490) Where the title to parsonage lands is in the minister as a sole corporation, on his death the title remains in abeyance until a successor is appointed.(491)

274. *Money, Control.*--Money raised by a Catholic congregation for the purpose of building a church does not come under the absolute control of the bishop or priest, although put into the hands of the latter for safe keeping. It is subject to the control of the congregation, although the members of the congregation refused to obey the command of the bishop of the diocese to consolidate with another church to which the priest was removed.(492)

275. *Church, Building, Removing.*--Where subscriptions were secured to build a church at a particular place as a memorial to a certain person, a congregation may be enjoined from tearing down the building and removing it to another place. (493) But a court of equity will not prevent the removal of a church where a majority of the congregation favors it, although a legal meeting had not been held to determine the matter.(494)

276. *Church, Use, Division.*--A church guild that erected a building adjoining a church for parish purposes, with the assent of the congregation, can not deny the authority of the church and use the building for other purposes.(495) But if members are improperly excluded from the use of the church property they must appeal to the courts for redress and can not resort to acts of trespass to gain entrance into a church.(496) A court of equity will compel persons having charge of the temporalities of a church, whether incorporated or not, to faithfully perform their trust and to prevent the diversion of the property from its original purposes. The court will not interfere in strictly religious matters.(497)

277. *Spanish Territory.*--When Alabama was a part of Spanish territory, a deed of land "to His Catholic Majesty for the purpose of building thereon a parochial church and dwelling-house for the officiating priest," the money being paid out of the royal treasury, did not constitute the King of Spain a trustee for the church or transfer to the church in equity a title to the lots.(498)

278. *Trust, Purposes, Doctrines.*--When a conveyance of a lot is made to certain persons of a religious society and their successors in trust for religious purposes, all the members become beneficiaries in equal degree notwithstanding some of them may have contributed larger sums than others.(499) Land conveyed to a church for valuable consideration belongs to the church, whatever change may take place in its religious doctrines; and if a minority secedes on the ground that they are the ones who retain the original tenets of the church, they can not take with them either the whole or pro rata share of the church property.(500)

279. *Control, Revenues.*--The trustees of a corporation of a church or of a religious society have entire control over the revenues of such body.(501)

280. *Leave to Purchase, Title, Canons of the Church.*--A congregation wanted to buy a church and priest's house, but the archbishop refused leave to purchase, but granted permission to keep the premises for religious purposes for a time. The members formed a society and bought and took title in the name of the "Lithuanian Benefit Society of St. Anthony." Then the archbishop wrote them a letter requiring the deed of the premises to be put in his name, which the congregation refused to do. A part of the congregation brought a suit in equity to enforce the transfer from the society to the archbishop. The court held that if the congregation was under the church and acknowledged its authority, the title must be settled by the canons of the church; otherwise, the majority of the congregation, in a duly called meeting, should determine where the title should be vested.(502)

281. *Cemetery, Authority.*--When a congregation that had title to a cemetery for many years entrusted the management and sale of the lots to the priest, he had thereby authority to create servitude, such as alleys to lots, which become binding on the congregation and all third persons.(503)

282. *Real Estate, Purpose.*--A church has no power to acquire and hold real estate for any purpose other than that of promoting the object of its creation, and any contract entered into for a purchase of real estate as a matter of speculation is *ultra vires* and void.(504)

283. *Limitation, Lands.*--A statute of the State prohibiting a religious society from holding more than twenty acres, applies to a single parish or congregation and not to the entire denomination when it consists of more than one congregation.(505)

284. *Conditions, Bequest, Deed, Time.*--Where property has been devised for a particular purpose or on certain conditions attached thereto, the law may be invoked to protect the fund according to the bequest.(506) And where a deed contained a clause that the lots should never be sold nor used in any other way except for the benefit of a specified Protestant Church, although the deed contained no clause of forfeiture, when the congregation sold the property the grantor was entitled to have the deed set aside and the title re-vested in himself. (507) And a grant made upon condition that a church be erected thereon, prevents the grantee from conveying it for other purposes without the consent of the grantor or his heirs.(508) But where a devise was made on condition that a church be built on the property within three years, the provision being a condition subsequent, a court has the right to extend the time.(509)

285. *Will, Forfeiture.*--The provision in a will or deed that land shall be used for purposes of a certain church, may create a trust for the benefit of the church only and not a condition the breach of which would work a forfeiture.(510) When a condition is put in a deed that it shall be forever used as a burial ground for the interment of bodies, it is doubtful whether the grantor and grantee together may change the uses of the property. Therefore, it is important in taking deeds to cemeteries to have no condition whatever, unless such conditions are desired. (511)

286. *Condition, Quit-Claim.*--After conveying land upon a specified condition, the grantor then gave a quit-claim deed, and the court held that that relieved the grant from the condition.(512)

287. *Bishop, Trust, Successors.*--A deed of land to the bishop of a church for a Protestant Episcopal church in fee simple, created a trust and on the death of such bishop the title passed to his successors.(513) Where a grantee in a deed absolute on its face, is in fact archbishop of the Roman Catholic Church for his diocese, its canons and decrees regulating the mode of acquiring and holding church property are competent evidence to show that the property is so held in trust for purposes for public worship and other charitable uses. And property so held by a Catholic bishop in trust for the diocese, or in trust for a congregation, school, cemetery, or asylum, for the separate use of each, is not chargeable with any part of the expenses of another one or for improving the church property generally in the diocese.(514)

288. *Trustees, Vacancy.*--When land is conveyed to certain persons as trustees of a church and their successors lawfully appointed, a court of equity will not step in to fill a vacancy but will leave that to be filled by the church in accordance with its discipline.(515) But an attempt to sell real estate of a religious society against the provisions of its charter, will be prevented by a court of equity.(516)

289. *Church, Majority, Change.*--When property is conveyed to a church having a well-known doctrine, faith, and practice, a majority of the members has not the authority or power by reason of a change of religious views to carry the property thus dedicated to a new and different doctrine.(517)

290. *Title, Harmony, Division.*--The title to church property in a divided congregation is in that part of the congregation which acts in harmony with the law of the denomination; and the ecclesiastical laws and principles which were accepted among them before the dispute began, are the standard for determining which party is right.(518) In other cases the division of church property, where there is a division of the congregation, depends upon its particular facts.(519) Where $400 was bequeathed to a Lutheran congregation in S----, there being at the time of the making of the will but one Lutheran congregation in the place, but subsequently a majority of the trustees and members with the pastor left the church and built a new one, the old church continued vested with the title to the property and all its funds.(520)

291. *Perversion, Misuse, Suit.*--Unless there is substantial departure from the purpose of the trust which amounts to a perversion of it, a court of equity will not interfere to prevent the misuse or abuse of a trust of a religious nature. In actions in the State court, if the church is not incorporated, an action should be brought in the names of the members collectively, and if they are too numerous to be all named, the suit may be brought in the name of one or more of them for the whole. The same rules apply to religious societies when sued. However, in some dioceses, particularly in the Catholic Church, the title to the church property is in the bishop and he thereby becomes an interested party who must be made either a plaintiff or a defendant.(521)

292. *Rights, Contracts, Torts, Crimes.*--Vested property rights, contracts, torts, and crimes, are usually subject to the laws of the State and the control and judgment of a church tribunal is seldom final. While the State courts have no ecclesiastical jurisdiction and can not revise or question ordinary acts of church discipline, they have the power to adjudicate conflicting claims of parties to the church property or the use of it.(522)

293. *Cemetery, Assessments.*--Where a lot was bought for the purpose of building a church but was used for a cemetery, and a church was built at another place and the deed to the lot was taken in the name of the trustees, the pastor and a member of the church corporation were not the proper parties to bring an action to restrain the State from selling the lot to pay the assessments for pavement, as they had no legal or equitable interest for the protection of which they could claim the interposition of a court of equity.(523)

294. *Burned, Revert, Vested.*--The fact that a church on lands donated to the parish, on condition of sustaining the church, burned down, the title did not revert to the grantor's heirs.(524) Also land granted a bishop for church uses, vested immediately in him and was not forfeited because it was not used for church purposes.(525)

295. *Abandoned, Revert.*--Land granted to trustees and their successors forever in trust to erect a Methodist church, according to its rules and discipline, which was used for such church for a long time and then abandoned and sold to parties who converted it into a blacksmith shop, did not thereupon revert in the absence of a provision to that effect.(526)

296. *Uses and Trusts.*--The chapter of the Wisconsin statutes on religious societies, although not included in the same title as the chapter abolishing all uses and trusts excepting as therein created, was not intended to prohibit the trusts expressly authorized by the former.(527)

297. *Trust Funds, Account.*--Where a member of the church received funds to invest in his own name for the benefit of the church, he will be obliged in a court of equity to give full account for the money and its profits.(528)

298. *Fund, Diverted, Split.*--A fund created for a particular purpose, as the education of children in the faith and doctrines of a denomination at the time the fund is created, can not be diverted from its original object.(529) Neither can such a fund be split up when a congregation is divided, but must be retained as created.(530)

299. *Church, Personalty.*--A church removed from its foundation and put on rollers was severed from the realty and became personal property.(531)

300. *Lease, Purposes.*--A religious literary society and scientific corporation has power to lease part of a building owned by it for theatrical and operatic purposes.(532)

301. *Salary, Lien, Equity.*--The church building and the land on which it stands have been held subject to the payment of a debt due for the salary of a pastor of the congregation owning such property.(533) A contractor is entitled to a lien on the church property for work done on the building.(534) A person who became liable for the debts of the congregation incurred in the purchase of church property, obtained relief in equity by subjecting the church property to a sale.(535)

302. *Bankruptcy, Creditors.*--There is no provision of law for a church corporation to make an assignment in bankruptcy. However, the church corporation may be sued and a receiver appointed to take possession of the property and sequester the assets.(536) But where assignments in bankruptcy and a sale and conveyance of church property are lawful, the church property may be assigned for the benefit of the creditors.(537)

303. *Jurisdiction, Process.*--In order to obtain jurisdiction where there are contentions between various persons claiming to be officers, the only safe rule is to serve the process on all those who are in the offices or claim the offices upon the occupants of which the papers must be served.(538)

304. *States, Property, Restrictions.*--Some States restrict the quantity and use of property that a religious society or church may hold. Other States have no restrictions; but nearly all the States have some statutory law on the subject, which is changed so frequently that it would be useless to give the provisions of such law in this work.(539)

305. *Land, Limitation.*--A statute of Illinois relating to Catholic societies contains no limitations on property rights, but it was held that the general law applied, and that an organization having ten acres could not acquire additional land by devise. A conveyance of land to a corporation after it has taken all the land allowed by law, is void.(540) In Kentucky where a church is limited to fifty acres and a devise was made to a church for the benefit of foreign missions, it was held valid under a statute providing that all devises for relief of aged, impotent, poor people, churches, or for any other charitable or humane purposes, shall be valid.(541) Maryland's peculiar law by which leave must be obtained from the Legislature for a conveyance of more than two acres of land, has been construed to give the Legislature authority to ratify a conveyance that otherwise would be void under the statute.(542) Also, it was held in the same case that a church might acquire more land, but that it would be restricted with regard to its use. A statute prohibiting a religious society from holding more than twenty acres of land applied to a single religious society and not to the denomination.(543) Where the territorial law provided that no religious corporation should hold real estate of greater value than $50,000, a receiver was appointed for the Mormon corporation.(544)

306. *Corporations, Bequests.*--Foreign religious corporations may be entitled to recover bequests made to them in some States; but the general rule is that a foreign religious society has no better right to take property by devise than a domestic corporation.(545) When the statute requires a conveyance to specify the purpose for which a religious society takes land, the failure to so specify renders the deed void.(546) But the Young Men's Christian Association was declared not within the limitation because it was not formed for pecuniary benefit and profit and was not under the control of any one denomination nor formed for religious worship.(547)

307. *Collateral Attack.*--A devise of land to a religious society which will increase the title beyond the amount that is allowed by statute, can not be attacked collaterally by a private individual.(548) It is for the State and not for the individual to make inquiry into excess on the part of a religious society in its accumulation.(549)

CHAPTER XXII.

RELIGIOUS SERVICES

308. *Worship, Discipline, Innovations.*--The denomination itself, according to its rules and regulations, determines what services shall form a part of its public worship. The inferior authority in the church has no right to violate the discipline by innovations. Whether or not devotional singing may be accompanied with instrumental music, must be determined by those who administer the discipline of the church.(550)

309. *Doctrines, Temporal Affairs.*--The fact that the congregation sells the pews does not give the owners the right to determine what doctrines shall be preached in the church, nor who shall preach them.(551) A majority of a local church can not change the faith of the church against the protest of the minority.(552) The corporation of the congregation is governed by the majority only in temporal affairs.(553) However, some of the Protestant churches are so independent that a vote of the congregation may transfer them from one denomination to another.(554)

310. *Contributions, Presbyterians, Methodists.*--Where certain persons by contributions built a church and the title was taken and held by the Presbyterians who permitted all other denominations to hold services therein, all of which was a condition of the subscriptions for establishing the church, when the Presbyterians sold out to the Methodists and they held it for their own exclusive use, those who contributed the money had the right to resort to the court to enforce their rights to worship in such church.(555)

311. *True Religion, Courts.*--Ordinarily the civil courts do not interfere where there is a question as to which of two or more parties is adhering to the true religious teaching of the denomination. If no question of property or civil rights arises, the court will not interfere.(556)

312. *Heresy, Injunction.*--Where a minister did not preach the doctrine and the entire system of Calvinistic theology received and taught by that denomination, he had no right to the pulpit of the church, and the court granted an injunction against his officiating therein.(557)

313. *Bequest, Sects, Condition.*--Where a bequest was made to erect a place of worship with the privilege for other sects to worship therein and forever to be used as such, the trustees in whom the title vested had no authority to sell without the consent of the grantor or his heirs; and the congregation having sold the church property and it having been thereafter used for a store, the grantor's heirs had a right of entry for condition broken.(558)

314. *Sexton, Undertaker, Authorities.*--The sexton who has charge of the church property may lawfully remove from the church an undertaker who, after being warned to desist and leave, persists in conducting the funeral in violation of rules prescribed by the authorities of the church.(559)

CHAPTER XXIII.

BEQUESTS, DEVISES, AND GIFTS

315. *Statutes, Wills.*--In some States a religious society can not take under a will, and a bequest of money to a church is void.(560) In Connecticut any devise to a religious corporation not expressly authorized by statute, is void.(561) In Maryland leave to devise land to a religious society must be obtained from the Legislature.(562) In all the States it is safest to consult and carefully follow the statute in drawing a will.

316. *Masses, Alabama.*--Formerly as a rule of the English common law, it was held that bequests and devises for the purpose of having Masses said for the soul of the deceased, were void as superstitious uses; but under Article 1 of the Amendments to the United States Constitution, and under similar provisions in the constitutions of the several States, the English rule does not prevail in the United States. However, Alabama adopted the English rule.(563) By reading the foot-note to the Alabama case, it will be found that a majority of the States hold that such bequests are lawful.(564) Even in Alabama if the bequest had been to a clergyman or a certain person and accompanied by a request to say Masses, the court might have allowed it.(565)

317. *Name, Bequest, Corporation.*--A mistake in a name does not render a bequest or a gift void if the person intended can be identified.(566) Also, a devise may be made to a corporation not yet organized and when it is organized the gift or devise will vest. During the interim, it will remain in abeyance.(567)

318. *Clergyman, Undue Influence.*--A clergyman who is a grantee in a deed from a parishioner, although deriving no benefit therefrom, has the burden of showing good faith in the transaction as the law presumes that he is guilty of undue influence. This presumption is further strengthened by proof of the enfeebled condition of the grantor by age and illness and his susceptibleness to influence. Where the property conveyed in trust for the parish was greatly in excess of its needs, the deed was set aside.(568)

319. *Contest, Secession.*--In case of a devise to a church which is claimed by two societies, it is the duty of the court to decide in favor of those who adhere to the ecclesiastical government of the church which was in operation at the time the trust was declared.(569) However, to maintain such action it must be brought by the proper parties.(570)

320. *Bequests, Membership.*--Bequests left to individuals on condition that they shall remain members of a certain church, can be obtained only by complying with such condition.(571)

321. *Conditions, Religious Tenets.*--In order to determine the conditions of a trust the religious tenets of the donor may be shown to aid in construction of ambiguous provisions.(572)

322. *Name, Uncertainty.*--A bequest to Georgetown University, in the District of Columbia, which was incorporated under the name of "The President and Directors of Georgetown College," is not void for uncertainty, as the only institution of learning in the District of Columbia is Georgetown College.(573)

323. *Future Uses, Uncertainty.*--A devise to a foundling or eleemosynary institution, whenever the Christians should create one which the trustees approved, is valid.(574) And a devise to the "First Christian church erected or to be erected in the village of Telfairville, in Burke county, or to such persons as may become trustees of the same," is good as a charitable bequest.(575) A bequest to a priest to hold in trust and pay over to the Sisters for the Poor, is valid.(576) A bequest for the care of a tombstone is valid in some States and not in others without a statutory provision.(577) A bequest to the bishop "to be by him used for Roman Catholic charitable institutions in his diocese," sufficiently describes the beneficiaries and is good.(578) Also, a bequest to Bishop England "in trust for the Ladies of the Ursuline Order residing in Charleston in the State of South Carolina," was held for "The Ladies of the Ursuline Community of the city of Charleston."(579) A bequest for Masses "to a Roman Catholic priest that shall succeed me in this place," was held void for uncertainty.(580) A bequest in trust to a bishop by name to sell and give the proceeds to a society named, is not a devise to the society, but to the bishop in trust.(581)

324. *Education, Priesthood.*--A devise or bequest to a clergyman of property to be used for the education of poor Catholic boys for the priesthood, was sustained in court as sufficiently definite for performance.(582)

325. *Charitable Trust, Cy-Pres.*--Equity will not allow a charitable trust to fail for want of a trustee, but will appoint one.(583) The doctrine of *cy-pres* as applied to charitable gifts and trusts, is not in force in Alabama, Connecticut, Delaware, Indiana, Maryland, Iowa, New York, North Carolina, nor Wisconsin; but seems to prevail in California, Illinois, Massachusetts, Missouri, Pennsylvania, and Rhode Island.

326. *Error, Ambiguity.*--Great latitude is allowed in charitable bequests, devises, and gifts, in proving *aliunde* the beneficiary intended where there is error in the name or a latent ambiguity.(584) The religion of the testator will be considered in proving intention.

327. *Dissolution, Resulting Trust.*--On dissolution of a religious society, the money collected or derived from the sale of property goes back as a resulting trust to the contributors.(585)

328. *Charity, Institutions.*--To determine what is a charitable trust, devise, or gift, it is necessary to particularly bear in mind the most comprehensive definition of charity. Legacies for schools, churches, libraries, cemeteries, the poor, hospitals, and numerous other eleemosynary institutions, have been sustained under charitable bequests when they otherwise would have failed.(586)

CHAPTER XXIV.

TAXATION

329. *Purposes, Exempt.*--Only church property that is actually used for church or charitable purposes, is exempt from taxation. Property held for its increase or profit is not exempt.(587) Land bought for a church on which no work on the church is yet begun, is not exempt from taxation.(588)

330. *Lot Isolated, Not Exempt.*--A lot isolated from the other property of the church of a congregation, is not exempt because the congregation intends to build a church thereon in the future, and actually did build a church thereon two years later.(589)

331. *Bishop's Residence, Hospital.*--Real property the title to which is in the archbishop in fee in accordance with the discipline of the Catholic Church, is not owned by a religious association so as to exempt it from taxation. The records do not show a trust for the diocese nor any other beneficiary. A court will not take judicial notice of the laws of the Catholic Church.(590) But property used as a hospital to care for the sick and wounded of all races and religions indiscriminately, with or without pay according to the ability of the patient, is a benevolent institution engaged in a work of charity, and comes under the law of tax exemption.(591)

332. *Parsonage, Rented.*--A parsonage owned by a congregation and used only as a residence for the clergyman is not exempt because of some part of it being also used for alleged religious services, to-wit: morning prayers of the children before school, a sewing society, and a meeting place for Sunday-school teachers.(592) However, a house and lot rented and kept by the minister was exempt from taxation.(593)

333. *Masonic Order, Charity, Elks.*--A charity which is confined exclusively to the members of the Masonic Order and their families or to the widows and children of deceased members or those who are directly or indirectly connected with the society, is not purely a public charity within the provisions of the constitution relating to the exemption of institutions of purely public charity from taxation.(594) And property held by the Elks for entertainment and to promote social intercourse was held not exempt.(595)

334. *Supporting Church, Mississippi.*--In the early ages of the States several of them had laws for taxing all the property in parishes laid out by the State for the support of Protestant churches. Gradually these laws were eliminated and at the present time there is probably no State excepting Mississippi that uses money for the support of a church. Maine changed her laws in 1821, and other States followed from time to time.(596) While those taxes were collected, no land within the parish was exempt in some States and in others the property of a nonresident was exempt.(597) In New Hampshire and Pennsylvania, a person could not be compelled to pay the taxes to a denomination of which he was not a member.(598)

335. *Appropriations, Contracts, Rent.*--Under the constitution of the United States, Congress can not make appropriations nor give aid to any denomination. Also, similar provisions are in many of the constitutions of the States. However, many cases arise out of contracts, which border upon these various rules, and in some States the constitutional provision of the State is such that the State Legislature may legislate concerning religions and give certain aid and support thereto. Paying rent to a congregation for a school-room is not an appropriation or aid to a church contrary to the constitution.(599)

Tax Provisions Affecting Churches

A. EXEMPT STATUS.

   1. Unlike all other §501(c)(3) organizations, a church is mandatorily presumed (under IRC §508(c)(1)):

     a. To qualify for exemption under §501(c)(3); and

     b. Not to be a private foundation. See §509(a)(1) and also §170(b)(1)(a)(i) relating to conductibility of donations.

   2. Which means that an ecclesiastical organization does not need to apply for a recognition of exempt status on Form 1023. And many do not apply. When might a church want to apply anyway? If it is part of a lesser known denomination or is an independent

church and/or needs to demonstrate proof of exemption for some other regulatory purpose.

3. Also note that the special election under §501(h) relating to lobbying expenditures of §501(c)(3) organizations is expressly inapplicable to churches, their integrated auxiliaries and any member of an affiliated group of organizations which includes a church. See §501(h)(5).

B. REPORTING AND EXAMINATION.

1. Churches are exempt from filing Form 990. See IRC §6033(a)(2)(A).

2. However, churches are not exempt from either the unrelated business income tax (§511) or the reporting requirements relating to UBIT (Form 990-T).

3. Church audits are subject to special rules of "reasonable belief" on the part of the IRS and advance notice requirements. See IRC §7611.

4. Unlike other organizations exempt from tax under §501(a), churches, their integrated auxiliaries, conventions or associations of churches need not notify the IRS in the event of liquidation. See IRC §6043(b)(1).

C. EMPLOYEE WELFARE PLANS.

1. The nondiscrimination requirements relating to group term life insurance plans do not apply to a "church plan" maintained for church employees. IRC §79(d)(7).

2. A church plan is also exempt from the continuation requirements applicable to a group health plan. IRC §4980B(d)(3).

D. EMPLOYEE RETIREMENT PLANS

1. Church plans are exempt from ERISA.

   a. Church plans are exempt from giving prescribed notices to employees, the preparation and distribution of a Summary Plan Description, certain filings with the federal Dept. of Labor, preparing annual reports to employees, and filing Form 5500.

   b. A church plan is subject to so-called "pre-ERISA" nondiscrimination standards, that is, standards in effect for retirement plans prior to September 2, 1974 (the "70% or 70/80% rule") as modified in 1996.

   c. Church plan status is determined by the status of the employer, not the plan participants. Thus, if a minister participates in a retirement plan sponsored by a non-church employer, the minister's participation will not make the plan a church plan. Similarly, a church plan may cover non-ministerial employees.

2. Definition of a church plan.

a. A church plan is defined at IRC §414(e), and includes plans maintained by organizations "controlled by or associated with" a church (church auxiliaries, etc.), as well as religious orders which carry out the functions of a church.

b. A complicating factor is that the tax code uses two distinct definitions for church with respect to employment and retirement plans; one under IRC §414(e) defining a church plan, and the other under IRC §3121(w), which defines wages for employment tax purposes. As an example, a theological seminary is treated the same as a church for minister's housing allowance purposes under IRC §107 and is arguably a church under IRC §414(e). However, the definition of church under IRC §3121(w) includes only elementary and secondary schools, not colleges or seminaries, and this is the definition which controls for purposes of IRC §457 deferred compensation plans.

3. Qualified plans under IRC §401(a).

a. A church plan is exempt from normal minimum participation standards, minimum vesting standards, and minimum funding standards. See IRC §410(c)(2)(B), 411(e)(2)(B) and 412(h)(4).

b. A church plan also has the benefit of limited exemptions with respect to other pension requirements, such as partial exemption from §401(a)(9), simplified rules for handling qualified domestic relations orders under IRC §414(p)(11), relaxed standards for defining a highly compensated employee under IRC §414(q)(9), etc. [This is not an exhaustive list of exemptions.]

c. Also, the tax on prohibited transactions concerning qualified plans does not apply to a church plan. IRC §4975(g)(3).

4. §403(b) Annuity Programs.

a. §403(b) plans, which may be adopted by any §501(c)(3) organization, are very popular with churches. But even here, churches are exceptional. For example, the nondiscrimination provisions of §403(b)(12) do not apply.

b. There are also a number of specialized or relaxed rules pertaining to churches in computing the limit on employee contributions and catch-up contributions. See IRC §402(g)(7) and §415(c)(7).

5. Section 457 deferred compensation plans which can be maintained by other tax exempt organizations cannot be maintained by a church or church-controlled organization, See IRC §457(e)(13).

E. CHURCH DEFINITION ISSUES.

1. Because of First Amendment religious freedom concerns, Congress has never passed any statute anywhere which defines what a church is (beyond saying "a church or convention or association of churches", which is like saying that the definition of a duck is "one or more

ducks").

2. The IRS, which apparently is unconstrained by the First Amendment, has nonetheless ventured where angels fear to tread, and has established criteria which, in its view, define a church as follows:

   a. A distinct legal existence
   b. A recognized creed and form of worship
   c. A definite and distinct ecclesiastical government
   d. A formal code of doctrine and discipline
   e. A distinct religious history
   f. A membership not associated with any other church or denomination
   g. An organization of ordained ministers
   h. Ordained ministers selected after completing prescribed studies
   i. A literature of its own
   j. Established places of worship
   k. Regular congregations
   l. Regular religious services
   m. Sunday schools for religious instruction of the young
   n. Schools for the preparation of its ministers.

3. The Tax Court, which is apparently unconstrained by the IRS administrative criteria, has adopted its own view, consisting of most of the same criteria compacted into 7 or 8 points. See, e.g., Pusch v. Commissioner, 39 T.C.M. 838 (1980) or Chapman v. Commissioner 48 T.C. 358 (1967).

4. What it all means is this: there is plenty of room for argument. Unless you have a clear case of a sham church (members and ministers are one and the same; members and/or ministers are all related; members 'donate' all of their income to the church, etc.), all of the definitional criteria can be argued, and indeed, bent, in favor of the church.

   a. Take the "Sunday School" criterion, for example. Must the religious instruction of children occur on Sunday, as opposed to Friday or Saturday or Tuesday? Of course not. Must it occur at the same time every week? No. Must it be undertaken with formal structure? Not necessarily. Does the organization teach kids at all? If so, that's good enough.

   b. Or take the "schools for ministers" criterion. Does a church have to have its own seminary (try to satisfy that expectation for an independent church)? No. Does the church train its ministers (whether by one on one mentoring or by attending 3rd party seminars)? If so, that's good enough.

   c. The other criteria can all be approached similarly.

CHAPTER XXV.

ELEEMOSYNARY INSTITUTIONS

336. *Poor, Institutions, Negligence.*--As hospitals, homes for the poor, and other eleemosynary institutions are supported by money given to charity, it would be a diversion of the trust funds if such institutions could be compelled to pay damages for negligence causing personal injury or death. The general rule is that the person causing the injury may be liable, but not the institution.(600) However, a charitable institution has been held liable for negligence of its manager to notify a nurse of the contagious nature of a case assigned to her.(601)

337. *Surgeon, Gratuitous Services.*--A charitable medical institution is not liable for the negligence of its surgeon in operating upon a patient gratuitously where such institution exercises due care in employing a surgeon deemed competent. The fact that besides such gratuitous services, medicine is taught therein for tuition fees and patients who are able to pay are charged a small fee for room, board, nursing, etc., but no fee from the patient to the doctor, does not change it from a charitable institution.(602) However, a hospital that is an adjunct to a medical school is liable.(603)

338. *Charitable Institution.*--An institution that limits its benefactions to the members of a particular denomination is, in the absence of a statute to the contrary, a charitable institution.(604) This rule has exceptions.(605)

339. *Charter, Real Estate.*--The trustees of a religious, literary, or other benevolent society, can not, irrespective of the powers granted by its charter, purchase and hold real estate under trusts of their own creation which will protect their property from creditors.(606)

340. *Mortmain, Title, Trust.*--The statute of mortmain was never in force in Pennsylvania, so a religious corporation can hold the legal title to land in trust for the heir-at-law of a testator who has devised it to the corporation in trust for uses that were void under the English law.(607) The only States that have statutes of mortmain are Mississippi and North Carolina. Yet in those States the statutes are somewhat different from the law of England.

341. *Public Institutions, Support.*--Benevolent and charitable institutions under a church are not public institutions, and moneys can not be appropriated for their support.(608)

342. *Nuns, Vows, Property.*--When joining a society of nuns, one of the vows taken was that all property should be held in common and whatever property was received after taking the vows should belong to the society. A person who left the order was not concluded from making claim for her property.(609)

CHAPTER XXVI.

SCHOOLS

343. *Parent, Education, State, Parochial Schools.*--The right of the parent to use judgment as to the proper necessaries of his child, including board, lodging, and education, is generally conceded. However, there must be no abuse of these parental rights, as the child also has rights that even a parent can not infringe. Therefore, the State may require a reasonable opportunity for the education of every child; and if the parent can not give it on account of his poverty, it is in the power of the State to take his child in charge and furnish him an education. The right of the State to make laws requiring a parent to send his child to school between certain ages, as from four to twenty-one years, is well settled. The question of the parent's being obliged to send his child to the public schools or being forbidden to send his child to a private or parochial school, is not settled in some States; but it is being settled in favor of the parent. The Kentucky constitution contains this provision: "... nor shall any man be compelled to send his child to any school to which he may be conscientiously opposed."(610) The right of the State to supervise or inspect private and parochial schools under the police power of the State can not be questioned.(611)

344. *Orphan Asylums, School Moneys.*--In 1850 the New York Legislature enacted a law as follows: "The schools of the several incorporated orphan asylums within the State other than those in the city of New York, shall participate in the distribution of the school moneys in the same manner and to the same extent in proportion to the number of children educated therein, as the common schools in their respective cities and districts." The court ruled that moneys devoted by the constitution to the State for the support of common schools could not be distributed under the act, for the reason that such asylums are not public schools; but moneys from other sources might be paid for the education of such orphan children in proportion to their number to those educated in the common schools of their respective cities and districts.(612) The schools kept by the Roman Catholic Orphan Asylum Society of the city of Brooklyn, are not common schools within the meaning of the constitution, and a provision of law that such schools should share in the distribution of school moneys raised by the State was void.(613)

345. *Contract, Direct Payment, Lease.*--No school of any denomination or sect is entitled to public moneys for its support, either by contract for the education of students therein or by direct payment from the government.(614) A school conducted by the Catholic Church in which religious instruction is given to Catholic children is a sectarian institution within the constitutional provision against using public funds for sectarian purposes; but public school money expended for such a school conducted by this school district could not be recovered by suit against the school officers.(615) Also, a school maintained as a charity under direction of trustees elected by the town where they must be of a certain religion, is not entitled to public moneys.(616) But the lease of a part of a parochial school building or the basement of a church for public school purposed does not violate the law.(617) In the States of Maine, Iowa, Massachusetts, Illinois, Ohio, Kansas, and Texas, the reading of the King James Bible and the singing of hymns and saying prayers have been held not sectarian.(618) But in Wisconsin, the court ruled the other way.(619)

346. *Teacher, Lord's Prayer, Exercise.*--"A public school teacher, who, for the purpose of quieting the pupils and preparing them for their regular studies, repeats the Lord's Prayer and the Twenty-second Psalm as a morning exercise, without comment or remark, in which none of the pupils are required to participate, is not conducting a form of religious worship or giving sectarian or religious instruction."(620) Substantially the same rule applies in Pennsylvania.(621) However, similar religious exercises conducted by Catholic teachers have generally been held sectarian and not permissible in public schools.(622)

347. *Ohio, Directors, Bible.*--The constitution of the State of Ohio does not enjoin nor require religious instruction or the reading of religious books in the public schools. The board of directors of a district has charge of the instruction and books to be used therein, and their official discretion will not be interfered with. Therefore, they were authorized to have the Bible read at the opening of the school.(623)

348. *Public School, Bible, Prayer.*--The committee having control of a public school may make a rule requiring the school to be opened by reading from the Bible and prayer every morning, and that each child shall bow the head during such prayers; that any scholar shall be excused from bowing the head whose parents request it; and when any scholar refuses to obey such rule and his parents refuse to request that he shall be excused, the committee may exclude such scholar from the school.(624)

349. *Text-Books, State.*--The State has the power to grant authority to the State Board of Education to select and prescribe text-books to be used in the public schools of the State.(625)

350. *Bible, Conscience, Constitution.*--The parent of a child expelled from the public school can not maintain an action against the school committee by whose orders it was done. In the same case it was held that a rule requiring every scholar to read a particular version of the Bible, though it may be against the conscience of some to do so, does not violate the letter or spirit of the constitution.(626)

351. *Schoolhouse, Sunday-School Purposes.*--The inhabitants of a school district have no right to use the schoolhouse for religious meeting on Sunday against the objection of any taxpayer in the district, notwithstanding that the officers of the district granted such right. A taxpayer may obtain an injunction against such use, although the injury to him be very slight, as he has no other remedy.(627) A district school board can not authorize the use of the schoolhouse for any other than school purposes.(628)

352. *Child, Immoral Character.*--The school committee in order to maintain purity and discipline, may exclude therefrom a child whom they deem to be of licentious or immoral character, although such character is not manifested in acts of licentiousness or immorality within the school.(629)

353. *Parents, Studies, Teacher.*--The requirement of a teacher that a scholar in grammar shall write English composition is a reasonable one, and refusal to comply therewith in the absence of a request from his parents that he be excused therefrom, will justify the expulsion of a scholar from school.(630) But when a parent selects certain studies that the law provides to be taught for his child to study, the teacher has no right to insist that the child shall take some other study and inflict punishment to enforce obedience.(631)

354. *Chastisement, Cruel.*--The chastisement of a scholar by the schoolmaster must not be excessive or cruel, but it should be reasonably proportioned to the offense and within the bounds of moderation.(632)

355. *Schoolmaster, Authority.*--Although a schoolmaster has in general no right to punish a pupil for misconduct after the dismissal of the school for the day and the return of the pupil to his home, yet he may on the pupil's return to school punish him for any misbehavior, though committed out of school, which has a direct and immediate tendency to injure the school and to subvert the master's authority. The fact that the master acted in good faith will not excuse him from damages for the punishment of a scholar where the punishment is clearly excessive and unnecessary. However, where there is a reasonable doubt the master should have the benefit of it.(633)

356. *Force, Assistance.*--And where a scholar in school hours places himself in the desk of the instructor and refuses to leave it on the request of the master, the master may immediately use such force and call to his assistance such aid from another person as may be necessary to remove the scholar. The same rule would apply to any one who is not a scholar and intrudes upon the school.(634)

357. *White, Unmarried.*--Before the adoption of the fourteenth amendment it was necessary in most States that in addition to the child being under twenty-one years of age, he must be of white blood and unmarried.(635) In Ohio, Negroes, Indians, and children of less than half white blood, were not entitled to the benefit of the school fund; and even where this would entirely exclude from school children not sufficient to form a district, still it was held that such children could not attend the white school.(636)

358. *Facilities, the Constitution.*--So long as abundant facilities are given for the education of all the children of a district, it is not a violation of the constitution of the United States to keep negro and white people separated. The same rule applies to courts.(637)

359. *Residents, Public Schools.*--Children in a German Protestant orphan asylum are not "children, wards, or apprentices of actual residents" in the district of the asylum, and therefore are not entitled to enter the public schools of the district.(638)

360. *Board, Majority.*--Two of the three members of a school board have no authority to act by themselves, and their individual agreement to dismiss a teacher is void. A school board can only act at a duly called meeting of the board, and then the majority vote duly taken decides.(639)

CHAPTER XXVII.

Religious Counseling: Duties of Disclosure

I. Confidentiality Requirements

  A. Generally.

    1. A counselor is generally obligated to keep secret the personal information disclosed by a client.

    2. The question of disclosure arises in two contexts:

      a. when the counselor can voluntarily disclose the client's secrets; and
      b. when the counselor can be legally compelled to disclose the client's secrets.

    3. The unauthorized disclosure of information may be actionable in some cases. Liability will tend to run both to the counselor and the employer/ministry.

  B. Social Workers

1. A social worker shall not disclose either:

    a. any portion of a communication made by the client to the social worker; or

    b. advice given by the social worker in the course of professional employment.

2. This privilege is not subject to waiver except when:

    a. the disclosure is part of the required supervisory process within the counseling agency; or
    b. except where waived by the client or a person authorized to act in the client's behalf.

3. This duty also applies to any employee or officer of an agency for whom the social worker is employed.

4. Certain nonspecific disclosures (for statistical purposes or to report the prospect or prognosis of a particular case without divulging a fact or revealing a confidential disclosure) may be made in connection with judicial or legislative requests.

5. The privilege must be claimed on behalf of a client unless the client authorizes disclosure or the privilege does not apply as provided by law.

6. Substantially similar disclosure duties apply to licensed professional counselors, psychologists, and marriage and family therapists.

C. Clergy

1. The clergy-penitent' privilege under Michigan law provides as follows:

No minister of the gospel, or priest of any denomination whatsoever, or duly accredited Christian Science practitioner, shall be allowed to disclose any confessions made to him in his professional character, in the course of discipline enjoined by the rules or practice of such denomination.

2. The case for confidentiality is clearest in a confessional setting.

    a. Counseling sessions involving standard clinical counseling methods, standard clinically recognized mental conditions, or non-clergy are not covered by the privilege.

    b. When the privilege does not apply, the counselor may be compelled to disclose the personal secrets of the client.

Comment: It is not clear what is meant by counseling which is "in the course of discipline" of a cleric. Most likely, this is not a reference to the narrow circumstance of when a person (the client) may be subject to formal church 'discipline,' but rather refers to any communications in the course of religious practice according to the rules and discipline of the church which the cleric is bound to observe. However, there is no case law interpreting this language.

3. For counseling activities performed by non-licensed and non-ordained counselors, or spiritual counseling performed by clerics which is non-confessional in nature, the issue of confidentiality will largely depend on the existence of an implied or express contract requiring confidentiality which is established at the commencement of the counseling relationship.

D. Domestic Violence Counselors

1. Michigan law also imposes a confidentiality requirement with respect to communications between a victim and anyone deemed to be a 'sexual assault or domestic violence counselor' in connection with the rendering of advice, counseling or other assistance to the victim.

Comment: Confidential communications and reports or working papers prepared in connection with a consultation are not admissible as evidence in any civil or criminal proceeding without the prior written consent of the victim (except is cases where a reporting of suspected child abuse or neglect is required).

    a. A 'sexual assault or domestic violence counselor' is anyone who "is employed at or who volunteers service at a sexual assault or domestic violence crisis center, and who in that capacity provides advice, counseling, or other assistance to victims of sexual assault or domestic violence and their families."

    b. A 'sexual assault or domestic violence crisis center' means "an office, institution, agency, or center which offers assistance to victims of sexual assault or domestic violence and their families through crisis intervention and counseling."

Comment: What is unique about this legal requirement, compared to other confidentiality requirements, is that it does not require the counselor to be licensed or a professional, for the duty to apply. Nor does it require the agency or ministry to hold itself out as a 'sexual assault or domestic violence crisis center.' All that is required for the duty to attach is that a counseling ministry include the counseling of victims or their families with respect to matters of sexual assault or domestic violence. The likelihood of any counseling ministry completely avoiding clients of this description is extremely remote.

2. Almost every counseling ministry conducted by a church is likely to qualify as a 'sexual assault or domestic violence crisis center' for purposes of this law.

II. Duties to Third Parties (Duty to Warn)

  A. Common Law Doctrine.

   1. Mental health professionals, because of their 'special relationship' with clients, have a duty to protect an intended victim of the client (including the client) from harm planned by the client if:

   a. the client has communicated a serious threat of physical violence; and
   b. there is a reasonably identifiable victim or victims.

   2. In such an event, the counselor must use reasonable care to warn and protect the victim(s) by communicating the threat to:

   a. the victim(s); and
   b. a law enforcement agency.

  B. Statutory Duty.

   1. If a patient communicates to a mental health practitioner who is treating the patient a threat of physical violence against a reasonably identifiable third person and the patient has the apparent intent and ability to carry out that threat in the foreseeable future, the mental health practitioner has a duty to:

   a. initiate proceedings to hospitalize the patient; or

   b. reasonably attempt to communicate the threat to the third person and the police; and

   c. if the third person is a minor or incompetent, to also reasonably attempt to notify Dept. of Social Services and the third person's parent or guardian.

   2. To Whom Applicable.

   a. This duty applies to any mental health professional, that is, psychiatrists, psychologists, social workers, professional counselors, and marriage and family therapists.

   b. The statute expressly states that this duty of disclosure does not violate any mental health professional's duty to keep client communications confidential.

   c. Clergy and lay people who are not professionally licensed are not subject to the duty imposed by this statute.

III. Child Abuse Reporting

   A. General Rule.

   1. All mental health professionals (psychologists, licensed counselors, social workers, marriage and family therapists, etc.) who have 'reasonable cause to suspect child abuse or neglect' have a duty to:

      a. "make immediately, by telephone or otherwise, an oral report, or cause an oral report to be made, of the suspected child abuse or neglect" to the Dept. of Social Services; and

      b. "within 72 hours after making the oral report, the reporting person shall file a written report" as required in the statute.

   2. 'Child abuse' means harm or threatened harm to a child's health or welfare by any person responsible for the child's health or welfare, or by a teacher or teacher's aide, "that occurs through non accidental physical or mental injury; sexual abuse; sexual exploitation; or maltreatment."

   3. 'Child neglect' means harm or threatened harm to a child's health or welfare by any person responsible for the child's health or welfare that occurs through:

      a. negligent treatment, including the failure to provide adequate food, clothing, shelter, or medical care; or

      b. placing a child at an unreasonable risk to the child's health or welfare by failure to intervene to eliminate that risk when that person is able to do so and has, or should have, knowledge of the risk.

   4. The duty to report suspected child abuse or neglect supersedes all privileges of confidentiality except for the attorney-client privilege.

      a. A person who fails to make a required report may be found guilty of a misdemeanor and may also be civilly liable for any damages caused.

   B. The identity of a reporting person is confidential subject to disclosure only with the consent of that person or by judicial process.

   1. A person acting in good faith who makes a report or cooperates in an investigation is immune from civil or criminal liability incurred by that action.

   2. This immunity extends only to acts done pursuant to law and does not extend to a negligent act that causes personal injury or death.

C. Spiritual or religious counseling by itself will not make anyone subject to the duty to report child abuse.

   1. However, a member of the clergy who is a mental health professional will not avoid the duty on religious freedom grounds.

   2. The duty also extends, in addition to mental health professionals, to any school administrator, school counselor or teacher, or regulated child care provider, including schools and child care centers maintained by churches.

IV. Recommended Protective Measures

   A. Proper forms should include, at a minimum:

   1. A client intake form should include:
      a) whether the counseling is intended to be spiritual or professional;
      b) whether the counselor is a licensed mental health professional, a member of the ordained clergy, both or neither;
      c) the identity of the counselor's supervisor and the nature of the supervision;

      d) brief summary of policies pertaining to information disclosure;
      e) an arbitration clause providing for problem resolution; and
      f) the signature of the client.

   2. Authorization to Release Information Form. Such a form should be separate from any other form and include:

      a) the uses and limitations of the information to be disclosed;
      b) the name and address of the church;
      c) the names or functions of the persons entitled to receive the information;

      d) the date after which disclosure is no longer authorized;
      e) a statement advising the client that they have a right to receive a copy of the authorization; and
      f) the signature of the client.

   3. Child Abuse Reporting Form.

   B. Proper procedures should include, at a minimum:

   1. All church personnel, especially counselors, and most especially those who counsel children, must be very carefully screened.
      a. Careful screening applies not only to employees, but also to volunteers, whose actions can result in liability to the church.

      b. References should be requested for all personnel, and verified (not merely filed).

c. Perform a personal interview and background check of every applicant for a position as a church staff member or volunteer.

d. Also, administer psychological testing to those staff and volunteers who will function as counselors.

2. All personnel, particularly all counselors, should be supervised and held accountable.

a. All non-licensed and non-ordained counselors should be supervised by someone who is licensed and/or ordained, depending on the type of counseling each person performs.

b. Further, licensed and/or ordained counselors should have a method by which they can keep each other accountable, not necessarily as supervisors, but as peers.

c. On-going training of all personnel is highly recommended.

3. Because of the potential spiritual, social and economic consequences that reporting may have, policies and procedures for dealing with child abuse reporting laws should be clearly defined, documented, and communicated to all staff.

4. Develop a list of licensed, competent mental health professionals who share the church's spiritual values and to whom the church can refer clients for evaluation and therapy. Offer routine written referrals to licensed mental health professionals to coincide with the purely spiritual counseling the church provides.

5. Have someone examine in detail existing office procedures, forms, and personnel policies so as to pinpoint any actual trouble spots peculiar to your ministry. An investment in some planning now will be worthwhile should a lawsuit come along.

PARENT AND CHILD

361. *Custody, Maternal Relatives, Father.*--A parent is entitled to the care and custody of his child if he is competent to transact his own business and not otherwise unsuitable. And the mere fact that the maternal relatives who have had the care of the child from its birth have become attached to it and desire to continue to care for it and are able to secure it better advantages than its parent, does not render the parent unsuitable to have its care and custody within the meaning of the statute. Also, the want of a sympathetic nature or cold reserve in a parent or the fact that he is away on business a great deal of the time, is not sufficient to render him unsuitable. But the right of the father may be lost or forfeited by his ill-conduct, gross ill-treatment, cruelty, or abandonment, or when his conduct and life are such as are injurious to the morals and interest of his child. When the father dies or forfeits his right for reasons already given, the mother, if alive, succeeds to all those rights, subject, however, to the same conditions as the father. And in the case of a child of tender years, the good of the child has to be regarded as the predominant consideration.(640)

362. *Mother, Illegitimate, Father.*--The mother has a right to the care and custody of her illegitimate child to the same extent that a parent has to his legitimate child.(641) The putative father on the mother's death succeeds to the mother's rights as against the maternal relatives and may secure the custody of the child by *habeas corpus*. This rule is different from the one that prevailed in the Roman law.(642) However, when the father has given bond for the care, support, and education of an illegitimate child, his right to the custody of the child may be superior.(643)

363. *Legitimatized.*--And when under a statute a child is legitimatized by acknowledgment or subsequent marriage, the father has the better right to its custody.(644) Usually there are many provisions in the statutes of the various States which substantially provide for the rights, relative and otherwise, of the parents and child in such cases.

364. *Punishment, Instrument, Murder.*--A parent or a person *in foro domestico* or *in loco parentis* may give reasonable corrective punishment with a fit instrument to a child. But if a parent or master whips a child so that it dies, he is guilty of manslaughter. And if he uses lethal instruments of punishment, he is guilty of murder.(645) Where a mother in anger threw a poker at one child and hit and killed another child, she was guilty of manslaughter.(646) The punishment always becomes unlawful when it is excessive, and drunkenness is no excuse.(647)

365. *Guardian, Religion, Courts.*--In England where a child was taken from the testamentary guardian, who after the death of the testator changed her religion from a Protestant to a Catholic, it was held thereby to be incompetent to continue as guardian.(648) And in New York it was held that where the father and mother were Catholics, the guardian must endeavor to bring the children up in that faith, as a guardian will not be permitted to proselyte wards.(649) But where a father who was a Catholic allowed his child to be brought up by a maternal aunt who was a Protestant, until the child was fourteen years of age, the father was not then entitled to the child's custody for the purpose of having it instructed in his own faith.(650) Courts will not interfere with the religion of a child, but will allow it to be brought up in the religion of its parents; however, the best interests of the child will be considered by the court without conceding everything else to its religion.(651)

366. *Convent, Consent.*--A daughter under age who entered a convent to become a nun without the consent of her mother, may, on a writ of *habeas corpus* on the petition of her mother, be required to leave the convent and return to her home.(652)

367. *Adoption, Rights, Duties.*--Persons of suitable age and circumstances to enter the marital relations, may adopt a child. When a married couple do not unite in adopting a child, the consent of the non-adopting spouse must be obtained. Also, if the child's parents are living, their consent is necessary unless they have lost their paternal rights by abandonment or divorce. The decree of adoption may be set aside for good cause. The adopted parent has all the rights over and duties toward the person of the adopted child that a natural parent has, including necessaries and religious training. Usually the child inherits from the adopted parents, but the adopted parents do not inherit from the child. The statutes on adoption are not the same in the several States, but they cover the subject and must be strictly followed.(653)

368. *Infancy, Manumission, Marriage.*--At common law a person is an infant until he is twenty-one years of age. Statutes have modified that rule so that girls in some States, and both girls and boys in others, may contract marriage at an earlier age without the parental consent. Generally, an infant can not contract marriage without the consent of the living parent or guardian unless the child has been manumitted. Where the boy was under the age of consent, but he falsely told the priest that he was of full age, his father had the marriage annulled.(654)

CHAPTER XXVIII.

HUSBAND AND WIFE

369. *Custody, Father.*--A husband is entitled to the custody of his wife against her father, and where a son-in-law killed his father-in-law in resisting the latter from taking his daughter out of his (the son-in-law's) house, the court held that it could not be more than manslaughter; and if it were necessary to kill to protect and maintain his wife, the defendant was not guilty.(655) But for good cause and without malice a parent may advise his child to leave spouse.(656)

370. *Corrective Authority, Services, Domicile.*--In America a husband gains no right to corrective authority over his wife. He can neither whip her nor use abusive language to her. The same rule applies to the wife, as they stand equal before the law.(657) However, a husband is entitled to all the services of his wife and a promise to pay her extra for housework can not be enforced.(658) Also, the husband has the right to determine their place of domicile, and if the wife unreasonably refuses to accompany her husband, it is desertion, for which he may obtain a divorce.(659)

CHAPTER XXIX.

INDIANS

371. *Indians, Citizens, Wards.*--There are a great number of statutory provisions concerning Indians, both in the United States statutes and in the statutes of the several States, most of which are not of great importance at the present time, as the Indians are confined to a few States. When they become citizens of the State in which they reside, their status is the same as other citizens; but so long as they remain in their tribal relations they are taken care of as wards of the Union.

372. *Schools, Cemeteries, Churches.*--In Oklahoma there are schools provided for them. When a tribe cedes 160 acres to the United States, it will give it a school for ten years, and as much longer as it deems necessary. Also, the Indians may have their own cemeteries, schools, and churches, where the Indians belong to the tribes, and they are allowed lands therefor.(660) In other States, under the general law, the money of Indian minors may be held in the treasury by the Secretary of the Interior and paid to parents and guardians in such sums and at such times as the Secretary in his discretion may determine. (661) There is no doubt that out of those moneys, parents might pay for their children at private schools.(662)

373. *Inspectors, Duties.*--Under the United States laws, inspectors are appointed to visit Indian agencies and investigate all matters concerning them and to examine all contracts and accounts with the Indians and make report thereon to the Secretary of the Interior. The contracts for support of religion, schools, and charitable institutions, come under their duties.(663)

374. *President, Trades.*--The President may cause Indians to be instructed in trades and agriculture and have them taught the elementary branches.(664)

375. *Commissioner, School, Rations, Bible, Sectarian.*--Another officer of great importance is the Commissioner of Indian Affairs, who has most to do with the education and schools of the Indians.(665) He may require parents and guardians to send children to school and withhold rations from them for failure so to do. Also, there is a fund under the control of the United States as trustee, with which he may make contracts for the education of Indian children at private schools.(666) However, the jurisdiction of the commissioner over Indian children does not extend to those off the reservation.(667) Among other provisions of the United States statutes is the following: "The Christian Bible may be taught in the native language of the Indians if in the judgment of the persons in charge of the school it may be deemed conducive to the moral welfare and instruction of the pupils in such schools."(668) The Bible continues its position among the Indians, but appropriations for the Church are cut off by the following provision: "It is hereby declared to be the settled policy of the government to hereafter make no appropriations whatever for education in any sectarian school."(669)

CHAPTER XXX.

JUVENILE COURTS

376. *Reformatories, Object, Liberty.*--During the past few years juvenile courts have been created for the purpose of committing children to reformatories. The proceedings are not criminal actions, but of an equitable nature.(670) However, as the object is to deprive the child of its liberty, the statute must be strictly construed and followed.(671) An infant can not waive a right.(672) If a child has been wrongfully committed or is wrongfully detained, the proper remedy for his discharge is a writ of *habeas corpus*.(673)

CHAPTER XXXI.

LIBEL AND SLANDER

377. *Confidential, Tribunal, Malice.*--The rule is that all confidential statements made to an officer or a tribunal of the church concerning a member in the course of church discipline and for the good of the church, if not made with malice, are privileged, and no action for libel or slander can be maintained therefor.(674)

378. *Member, Officer, Councils.*--But slanderous or libelous statements made concerning a person not a member of the church or made concerning a member of the church to another member who is not either an officer or in the councils of the church, are actionable and the person making or publishing such statements is liable for damages. Also, a person who repeats a libel or slander may be liable as though he were the originator.(675)

379. *Official Communication, Privileged.*--An official communication between authorities of the church or an authority and a member of the church concerning a church matter or church members and not made in malice, is privileged.(676)

380. *Priest, Pastoral Duties.*--Where a priest published from the altar that "Peter Servatius is excommunicated, because he laid hands on the priest to put him out of the church, and he has no more benefit of the prayers of the church. I will not pray for him, and consider him a lost sheep and withdraw all my pastoral blessings from him. If he die, the burial rights of the church will be denied him," such remarks were held defamatory, unless they were spoken in the proper discharge of the priest's clerical and pastoral duties and without malice; and the case should have been submitted on the evidence to a jury.(677)

381. *Church Record, Excommunication.*--An entry of a church record that "A report raised and circulated by A. B. against Brother C., stating that he made him pay a note twice, and proved by A. B. as false," is libelous.(678) But an entry of excommunication of a member made in the record and shown to other members, is not libelous, the latter being properly a part of the record and the former extraneous.(679)

382. *Will, Libel, Action.*--The will of a priest contained a statement that a relative had received $300 from him for clothing, maintenance, education, etc., and promised to repay it, but paid no part of it. Then testator bequeathed said $300 to two legatees to collect for their own use. The relative filed a petition asking the estate of the priest to be held liable for a libel in the sum of $50,000 and the court held that as the right of action did not accrue until after the death of the testator, there was a right of action against the estate. As the case never got beyond the probate court, its authority is doubtful.(680)

383. *Language, Insane, Good Faith.*--Unless the language is used by the bishop in the line of his duty, a statement that a priest is irresponsible and insane, that he was removed from his position of priest for good reason, and that he has been guilty of ecclesiastical disobedience, is slanderous *per se*. To make a communication between a bishop and priest privileged it must have been spoken in good faith and in belief that the speaking of it came within the discharge of the bishop's duty.(681)

384. *Rector, Bigamy, Tobacco, Liquor.*--In a case where the rector of an Episcopal church called upon a man charged with bigamy and after a private conversation the minister wrote a letter to the district attorney on behalf of the prisoner, it was held not privileged because it was not made in confidence of the relation and was not kept as a secret.(682) A letter from a church member of one congregation to the elders of another congregation advising them of the unfitness of a clergyman appointed to the latter parish, and stating that he used tobacco and liquor, that he was an untruthful man, and that his family was no credit to the community, was quasi-privileged; and in the absence of proof that the charges were false and malicious was not actionable.(683)

385. *Newspapers, Criticisms, Priest.*--A newspaper has a right to publish criticisms of the conduct of a priest in certain services held in his church if no false statement of facts is given, since such conduct is a proper subject of discussion; and if such article contains a statement that if certain published accounts of the conduct of the priest are true he acted in an improper manner, etc., it is not libelous because such facts are not true, as it is not an affirmation of the truth thereof. Where the alleged libel was published in a foreign language and the correctness of the translation was disputed, it was an error for the judge to instruct the jury that if the translation introduced in evidence was correct, the defendant was liable, since plaintiff's right to recover should not be made to depend on the absolute accuracy of the translation.(684)

386. *Clergyman, Discipline, Tribunals, Testimony, Argument.*--What a clergyman says in the administration of the discipline of the church or what is said in tribunals to enforce discipline of the church, including testimony and legitimate argument within the scope of the case, if said in good faith and without malice, is not actionable in the civil courts.(685)

387. *Physical Discipline, Imprisonment, Courts.*--A clergyman who claims to have been slandered by a parishioner can not administer physical discipline nor put the offender under restraint without leaving himself liable for damages for assault and battery or false imprisonment. If the clergyman desires to treat the charge as a church matter, he must go into the church tribunal; otherwise, his proper course is to bring an action for slander in the State court.(686)

388. *Sermon, False Statement, Crime.*--A clergyman may, by words used in a sermon, slander a member of his congregation. However, if he makes no false statement and does not falsely or maliciously charge a crime, what he says in the way of discipline is privileged.(687) The meaning of the words "she is a dirty, vile woman," can not be extended by innuendo.(688)

389. *Charges, Robbed, Hypocrite.*--Charges that a person has robbed a church or has stolen from a church, are actionable.(689) Also, charging a person with being a hypocrite and using the cloak of religion for unworthy purposes, is slanderous.(690)

390. *Investigation, Probable Cause.*--When a member of a church consents to an investigation on complaint before a person who is not a member, if the complaint was made on probable cause and not under the pretense of exposing the defendant to scorn or obloquy, he could not subsequently bring an action for libel.(691)

391. *Sacraments.*--To publish of a person that he has been deprived of the sacraments of the church to which he belongs, is libelous.(692)

392. *Obituary, Tolling Bell.*--To falsely and maliciously publish an obituary notice of a person living, is good ground for an action for libel.(693) However, a complaint that a church tolled its bell to announce the death of a member, and did report him dead when he was actually living, and that it was all done for the purpose of annoying, harassing, and vexing the person and his family, was held not sufficient to support an action for libel. The latter case is doubtful law.(694)

393. *Newspaper, Profane Swearer.*--A newspaper in a notice of the death of a church member has the right to state that he was a profane swearer, if such was the case.(695)

394. *Business or Property, Special Damages.*--A company incorporated for the purpose of transacting business which would include hospitals, schools, and industrial institutions, may maintain an action for libel the same as an individual for any words affecting its business or property, if special damages are alleged and proved.(696)

395. *Justification, Repeating.*--It is no justification that libelous matter had been previously published by a third person, that the name of such person was disclosed at the time of repeating the libel, and that the person who was repeating it believed all the statements in the libel to be true.(697)

CHAPTER XXXII.

CRIMES

396. *Sins, Crimes, Discipline.*--Crimes are offenses against the civil law. The fact that the church organization may try and punish a member for sinning, or acquit him, has nothing whatever to do with the administration of the criminal law of the State. Therefore, a member may be arrested and tried for any offense before or after the ecclesiastical tribunal has taken action in the matter. But there are certain crimes of a religious nature of which the civil law assumes jurisdiction and punishes, such as blasphemy,(698) disturbing religious meetings,(699) etc. Most of those laws are statutory and depend wholly upon the statute of the State where the crime is committed.

397. *Profane Language, Smoking, Disturbance.*--Rude behavior or profane language if audible,(700) smoking in the church or during services,(701) cracking and eating nuts in church,(702) and fighting near the church so as to disturb the services, are violations of the law.(703) A father's taking his child out of the church with violence is a disturbance of the meeting.(704) The disturbance of any member of the congregation assembled for religious worship is a violation of law.(705) A sentence of $100 fine or one year's imprisonment in the penitentiary, is not excessive or cruel or unusual punishment on conviction for disturbing a meeting.(706)

398. *Sunday-School, Church.*--An ordinary Sunday-school where the Bible and religious precepts are taught, is a church within the law.(707)

399. *Private School.*--A person may be punished under the statute for willfully disturbing a private school kept in a district schoolhouse for instruction in the art of writing.(708)

400. *Disturbing a Religious Meeting.*--Under a statute against disturbing a religious meeting, it has been held that it should define what disturbance is punishable.(709) Also, mere want of attention or observance of ceremonies, as standing or kneeling at times, is not a violation of the law.(710) Neither is singing out of time, unless done purposely,(711) nor performing a proper duty, such as objecting to a silenced clergyman's conducting the services.(712)

401. *Common Law, Offense, Statutory Law.*--If there is no statutory provision, in those States where the common law prevailed before the admission of the State to the Union the offense is punishable under the common law.(713) And even in States where there is a statutory law on the subject, a person may be convicted at common law.(714)

402. *Services, Violation, Time.*--The nature of the services and the discipline of the denomination may determine whether there is a violation of the law. Usually the disturbance may occur at any place the congregation is assembled, and at any time when any part of the congregation is assembled for religious services or business.(715)

403. *Force, Priest, Preserve Order.*--A congregation may use sufficient force to remove a disturber.(716) A Catholic priest who is the conductor of religious services and master of ceremonies within his church has the right to preserve order and to remove by force, if necessary, any person who disturbs his services.(717)

404. *Interrupt, Liquors, Traffic.*--There are statutes in most of the States making it a penal offense to interrupt or molest any assembly or meeting of the people for religious worship, or to sell intoxicating liquors or other articles of traffic within a certain distance of any camp-meeting or other religious assembly, except at a place of business regularly established prior to such meeting or assembly and not with intent of evading the provisions of the law.(718)

405. *Theory, Blasphemy, Crime.*--On the theory that the United States is a Christian nation, blasphemy is held to be a crime.(719) Infidels naturally claim that it interferes with their rights. However, there is no more interference with the private rights of the infidel than there is with the private right of the Mormon who is forbidden to violate the laws of the country by having a plurality of wives; and it has been held that any words importing imprecation for divine vengeance may constitute profane cursing or blasphemy.(720)

406. *Religion, God, Ridicule, Virgin.*--Words vilifying the Christian religion,(721) denying God or the final judgment,(722) and profane ridicule of the Holy Scriptures or of Christ,(723) are usually punishable. Also, the use of vile words applied to the Virgin Mary is blasphemy.(724)

407. *Profanity, Proof, Excuse.*--The profanity must be in the hearing of some person.(725) Every time a person profanely swears by taking the name of God in vain is a separate offense.(726) The prisoner's confession is sufficient proof; otherwise the prosecution must show that the offense was committed and some

one heard the words.
Drunkenness is no excuse.(727) Punishment by fine or imprisonment is not in violation of the constitution of the State or of the United States.(728)

408. *Sunday, Business, Fishing.*--The offenses against the Sunday law are so numerous that it would be almost impossible to review them within the limits of this work. Of course, the carrying on of a man's ordinary business is a violation of the Sabbath laws. But in some States selling cigars,(729) a butcher selling meat, (730) and even selling soda water,(731) and ice cream,(732) as well as fishing, traveling, driving, using a slot machine,(733) and almost every other imaginable act excepting going to church, has at some time and in some State been declared a violation of the law, and a penalty imposed therefor.
In California,(734) Tennessee,(735) and Washington,(736) men may be shaved on Sunday. In some other States it has been held that running a barber shop on Sunday is a violation of the law.(737)

409. *Charity, Necessity, Benefit, Pleasure.*--However, doing works of charity and works of necessity usually are exempt. What is a work of necessity is a question of law. Charity includes whatever proceeds from the sense of moral duty or a feeling of kindness and humanity, and is intended wholly for the purpose of the relief or comfort of another, and not for one's benefit or pleasure. (738)

410. *Contracts, Marriage, Notice.*--The common law made no distinction between Sunday and any other day as to making contracts, but it prohibited holding court. In this country the statutory law invariably prohibits any but works of necessity or charity to be done on Sunday. But marriage settlements,(739) publication of statutory notices on Sunday,(740) and promises to marry, have been held legal.(741)

411. *Funeral, Physician, Subscriptions.*--To attend a funeral, to employ an undertaker, or a physician, on Sunday, has been tested in the courts, and finally decided to be works of necessity or charity and not a violation of the Sunday law. Also, subscriptions made for church purposes and in works of charity on Sunday have been held legal and binding.(742)

412. *Jews, Seventh-Day Observers.*--In several of the States it has been held that Jews and Seventh-Day observers of the Sabbath must obey the Sunday law. (743) However, in many States there is a statute expressly exempting people who keep the seventh day of the week; but still they sometimes have a provision, unless "he shall willfully disturb thereby some other person or some religious assembly on said day."

413. *Societies, Secular Work.*--Business meetings of benevolent and church societies for benevolent or church work may be held on Sunday. Even the constitution of such societies may be amended on Sunday. However, secular work that does not come strictly under the functions of such societies would be unlawful.(744)

414. *Sunday, Begins, Ends.*--Usually people believe they know what the word Sunday means, when it begins, and when it ends. Christianity usually recognizes the time from midnight to midnight as Sunday, and that is the usual time recognized by law.(745) But the solar day only,(746) or from midnight to sunset, (747) give us a variety which may not be complete. Also, we have the further anomaly of a note made at 2 o'clock on Saturday night, being held valid.(748)

415. *Religious Liberty, Law.*--The constitutional guarantee of religious liberty is not violated by enforcing the Sunday law.(749)

416. *Necessaries, Doctor.*--As a parent or husband is obliged to furnish necessaries for his children and wife, when medical treatment becomes necessary, he is liable for manslaughter for failure to do his duty, even in case of religious disbelief in the efficacy of medicine. Courts are not inclined to make any distinction as to religious belief, and the prevailing rule in this country is that the parent is liable if he negligently allows his child to die when it might have been saved by the services of a doctor.(750)

417. *Christian Healer, Consent.*--A Christian healer can not be held liable except under a State law. One who consents to treatment has no action for damages unless there is a failure to exercise the care and skill of a Christian Scientist. This rule might not apply to one incompetent to consent to a contract. (751)

418. *Politics.*--A minister who had been expelled by his congregation for voting the Democratic ticket, had some of the members of the church arrested under the election laws for intimidating a voter. The court held that as he "suffered no pecuniary loss, personal injury, or physical restraint," no crime was committed. (752)

419. *Mail, Obscene Language.*--Under the United States postal laws against sending "obscene, lewd or lascivious" books or papers through the mail, a person can not be convicted without proof that the matter is obscene, lewd, and lascivious, as the word "or" should be construed to mean "and." Also, the court held that a newspaper article on the doctrine of the Immaculate Conception written in coarse and obscene language that offended the religious sentiments of the people, but had no tendency to induce sexual immorality, did not render the newspaper unmailable nor the publisher guilty under the United States statutes. The court says: "Those parts of the article most relied upon to sustain the charge, though ostensibly a discussion of a religious subject, are couched in language not quite suitable for insertion in a judicial opinion, however well adjusted to such applause as might be expected from taste of a certain degree of degradation."(753)

420. *"Fair," Chances, Gambling.*--A church "fair" at which chances are sold, drawings had, or any game of chance permitted, is illegal and may be punished as gambling.(754)

CHAPTER XXXIII.

CEMETERIES

421. *Statutes, Land.*--There are sufficient statutory provisions on cemeteries to make a large book, and the frequent changes made in such laws render a full statement of the law impossible. The statutes against locating cemeteries near cities, dwellings, etc., should be carefully examined before buying land therefor. (755)

422. *United States, Jurisdiction.*--The jurisdiction over the United States cemeteries is in the State where the cemeteries are located unless such jurisdiction has been ceded to the United States.(756)

423.. *Tombstones, Soldiers.*--The United States will erect tombstones at the graves of soldiers who served in the Civil War, in all cemeteries where their graves are unmarked. Wherever the United States has jurisdiction over cemeteries, it has made it a criminal offense punishable by fine or imprisonment to deface a tombstone.(757)

424. *Indigent Soldiers, Tombstones.*--Most of the States have statutes providing for the burial of indigent soldiers and for putting tombstones at their graves. The attention of relatives of deceased soldiers should be called to it.

425. *State Authority.*--The State Legislature has authority to control cemeteries or delegate that authority to some one else, and afterward to transfer it to a different person.(758)

426. *Maryland, Two Acres.*--Although the declaration of rights of the State of Maryland restricted the sale of lands for a cemetery for a church to two acres, the Legislature has power to grant leave to a cemetery association to take title to more land. And where the trustees bought twelve acres of land for a burial ground and a subsequent act of the Legislature authorized the enlargement of the cemetery not to exceed twenty-five acres, the title to the excess of the valid purchase was ratified and the title vested in the trustees.(759)

427. *Consent, Application.*--Where a statute provides that no cemetery shall be laid out without first obtaining the consent of the municipal authorities thereto, a written communication signed by the officers of an incorporated society is sufficient application; and a motion granting consent adopted by the city council is sufficient action on its part to comply with the statute.(760)

428. *Charter, Ground, Members.*--An application for a charter to incorporate a cemetery need not specifically locate the ground.(761) The charter or the articles of incorporation, or by-laws made under them, generally determines who shall be members of the corporation. And where every owner of a lot signing the constitution and by-laws becomes a member, the trustees can not vote on the unsold lots.(762)

429. *Police Power, Trespass, Burial.*--Under our laws the State, by reason of its police power, has control over the cemeteries within it. However, that power has generally been very favorably exercised. Laws both civil and criminal have been enacted to protect cemeteries from invasion and trespass and to protect tombstones from injury.(763) When authorized by the Legislature a city may make a by-law prohibiting burial within its limits, notwithstanding that the cemetery has been constantly used for over one hundred years.(764) Also, the city has authority to protect and regulate the use of a cemetery.(765)

430. *Dwelling, Limits.*--Most of the States provide that no cemetery shall be laid out within a certain limit of a dwelling. But after the cemetery is established a man can not have it moved when he puts up a dwelling within the limits or where he consented to the cemetery at the time it was established.(766)

431. *Well, Pollution.*--And where a man had built a dwelling near a cemetery, it was not good ground for him to prevent the enlargement of the cemetery by showing that it might destroy his well. The court questions whether there is any legal ground for complaint for the pollution of subterranean waters when caused by the proper use without negligence of the adjacent premises.(767) Additional lands may be obtained under the law of eminent domain by condemnation.(768)

432. *Exempt, Execution, Mortgage.*--The statutes in most of the States exempt the tombstones and lots in a cemetery from sale on execution.(769) Also, a cemetery lot can not be sold under mortgage after bodies have been buried therein, as any one may be arrested for desecration of graves.(770)

433. *Public, Regulation.*--The right to bury in a public cemetery is a privilege or license that is subject to municipal regulation, and revocable whenever the public necessity requires it.(771)

434. *Nuisance, Public Health, Disease.*--A cemetery is not a nuisance *per se*, but if it is proved that the burial of dead bodies in a certain cemetery does injure the public health and is a fruitful source of transmission of disease, the State may prohibit such burial at certain places within cities or adjacent to dwellings. But unless authorized by the Legislature a council has no right by ordinance to provide that no one shall be buried within half a mile of any habitation or public thoroughfare.(772) And where the Legislature authorized a city to remove the bodies interred and allow streets through the land, it had authority to do so.(773)

435. *Devise, Easement, Rules.*--The general rule of law is that a man can not devise away a cemetery lot in which members of his family are buried. He owns only a license or at the most an easement which is subject to the rules of the cemetery association and the police power of the State. However, there are some exceptions.(774)

436. *Conditions.*--A condition in a deed that the lot can not be sold, assigned, or transferred without consent of the cemetery corporation, is as good and binding as in any other conveyance of real estate.(775)

437. *Inherits, Right.*--Where a son inherits from his father the right to burial in a cemetery lot, he has the right to remove and inter therein the bodies of his grandmother and sister who had been buried elsewhere.(776)

438. *Certificate.*--A certificate was issued for the burial of Dennis Coppers in the following form:
"Office of Calvary Cemetery, New York, December 1, 1873.
RECEIVED from Mr. Dennis Coppers, seventy-five dollars, being the amount of purchase money of a plot of ground 8 feet by 8 feet, in Calvary Cemetery.
D. BRENNAN, Superintendent of Calvary Cemetery.
4 Graves, 5, 6, 7, 8, Plot D, Section 7, Range 35."

439. *Freemason, Title, Right.*--Prior to 1879, the mother, wife, and other relatives of Coppers, who were Roman Catholics, were buried in the lot covered by the deed given in the last paragraph. Coppers, who was a Freemason, died in August, 1879, and his funeral services were held under the auspices of the Masons from an Episcopal church, as directed in his will. The rules and doctrines of the Church forbid the burial in consecrated ground of the body of one who was not a Roman Catholic or who was a member of the Masonic fraternity. The Church authorities refused to allow Coppers to be buried in the cemetery, and application was made by his relatives for a writ of mandamus to compel his interment therein, they having deposited the necessary money to pay all the expenses. The court held that the certificate delivered to Coppers was not a conveyance nor a grant and did not vest title to the land in him, and that the cemetery could not be compelled to execute and deliver to him an absolute conveyance of the lot. His only right under the certificate was the use of the lot for burial purposes subject to and in conformity with the established rules and bylaws of the corporation in so far as they were not in violation of any law. It is the tacit understanding, when a person applies for a burial lot in a cemetery of the Catholic Church, that he is either a Catholic and as such is eligible to be buried therein, or that he applies in behalf of those who are in communion with the Church.(777)

440. *Lots, Fee.*--If the cemetery association sells 400 lots to one man and makes a conveyance in fee thereof, it is bound thereby.(778)

441. *Deed, Privilege, Heirs and Assigns.*--No formal deed is necessary to confer exclusive right to the use of a cemetery lot for burial purposes.(779) And certificates of lots issued by a corporation convey no title to the land, as they are not in the form necessary to constitute a conveyance of land. Their only effect is to grant the privilege of interment so long as the ground continues to be used for the purposes of burial.(780) A deed of a cemetery lot "to him, his heirs, and assigns forever," gives only an easement in the freehold, and does not give title to the soil, and is subject to changes made necessary by altered circumstances. (781)

442. *Access, Purposes.*--Title to a cemetery lot gives the right of access to it for the usual purposes, including putting up monuments.(782)

443. *Monuments, Inscriptions, Drunkenness, Non-Baptized, Strangers.*--The plaintiff obtained from the defendant a deed, which, among other things, contained the following conditions: "that such lot shall not be transferred without the consent of the trustees; shall be subject to the regulations made, or to be made, in the care and management of such cemetery by the trustees, who shall also have the right to prevent the erection of offensive and improper monuments or inscriptions thereon, and shall retain the right to enter any lot for the removal of anything objectionable; that no remains shall be deposited therein for hire; and that persons dying in drunkenness, duel, or by self-destruction, non-baptized, non-Catholic, or otherwise opposed to the Catholic Church, shall not be therein interred." The plaintiff had buried his father and one of his children in the lot, and brought his wife's remains there for burial. Upon the arrival of the funeral, two small coffins of strangers, one of which bore the name "John McDonald," which the grave-digger had taken up, were at the side of the grave. There was nothing to show how those bodies came to be buried there. The plaintiff brought suit for damages against the cemetery association. The court held that the cemetery association was liable and that the defense that it was a public charitable organization could not be sustained.(783)

444. *Use, Forfeited.*--When a deed is made of land for the use of a cemetery only, it will be forfeited by using it for a school.(784)

445. *By-Laws, Member, Burial.*--Where a by-law of a church association provides that any member who pays one dollar to have his name entered in the record shall be entitled to a burial lot, a member who had paid one dollar to the committee of the church before the adoption of such by-law but had ceased to be a member of the congregation, has no right to a burial lot.(785)

446. *Adverse Possession.*--If the original title to a cemetery is defective, the title may become good by adverse possession.(786)

447. *Improvements.*--The owner of a lot, unless some rule of the cemetery association or law of the State is to the contrary, may improve it as he sees fit so long as he does not injure the property rights of another.(787)

448. *Trespass, Injunction.*--An action for damages *quara clausum fregit*, can be maintained by a relative against any one who trespasses upon a grave of a person lawfully interred.(788) Also, a relative may enjoin by suit in equity, on behalf of himself and others equally interested, interference with graves in his cemetery lot.(789)

449. *Roads, Alleys.*--Most of the laws relating to highways apply to cemetery roads and alleys, excepting that when a road or alley in a cemetery is vacated the land reverts to the cemetery instead of becoming parts of the adjoining lots.(790) In most of the States a road can not be laid out through or take a part of a cemetery.(791) But a public highway may be established through a cemetery by user, the same as over other lands.(792)

450. *Abandoned, Bodies.*--When a cemetery has been abandoned, those who have relatives buried there may incorporate it for preservation.(793) Also, a corporation may change its cemetery and remove the bodies interred therein.(794)

451. *Two-Family Lot, Control.*--Where a lot is owned jointly by two families, one burying in the north half and the other in the south half, the family burying in the north half can not prevent the burial of a member of the other family in the south half, if entitled to be buried in that cemetery.(795)

452. *Burying Dogs, Removal.*--A person who has a lot in a cemetery has no right to bury any but human bodies therein, and one who has buried a pet dog in her lot may be compelled to remove it.(796)

453. *Stranger, Protest, Kin.*--One member of a family can not authorize the burial of a stranger in a family lot where his parents are buried and against the protest of any other relative of equal or nearer degree of kin.(797) When an owner of a lot has consented to the burial of a body therein, he can not afterward remove the body or deface the tombstone, and to do so would be a criminal offense.(798) When a lot is sold to one person, the cemetery association has the right to limit interments to members of the family owning the lot. However, where there is nothing concerning it in the laws or rules of the association, it might be different.(799)

454. *Association, Bishop, Stipulation, Certificate, License, Revocable.*--The

Germans of Cincinnati formed an association and purchased ten acres of land for a cemetery "for German immigrants, their families, and relatives, of Cincinnati and its vicinity, who might be members of the Catholic Church and in accordance with the doctrine, discipline, usage, and ceremonies of the same." They incorporated with fifteen trustees to be elected annually. Before he would bless the cemetery, the bishop required and the committee stipulated with him in writing the following: That the rules of the Catholic Church should always be faithfully observed in this chiefly: First, that no one should be buried in the ground who had not been baptized or who died out of communion of the Catholic Church, to which the bishop or in his absence the clergy of the German Catholic Church or churches, should be the judge; second, that no poor person should be denied a place therein because his parents were unwilling to pay; third, that any money accrued from the ground should be expended for pious uses and specifically for the relief of the German Catholic poor; fourth, that the remains of persons interred in Catharine Street burial-ground might be removed to the new ground. The bishop subsequently closed the cemetery as a place for burial of Catholics because the congregation had violated the stipulation: "First, by admitting those to burial who died out of the communion of the Catholic Church; second, by refusing to poor persons the right of burial; third, by expending the funds of the association in other than pious uses and relief of the poor." The court held that the corporation had authority to determine that the cemetery should continue to be used as such, but the conditions might be enforced by any one interested.(800) Also the question was brought before the court in a case where a man had fallen away from the Church, and the court held that the certificate was a mere license giving no property rights, and revocable; and that the question as to whether the party to be buried therein was in communion with the Church, was one over which the Church itself had exclusive jurisdiction.(801)

455. *Rules, Diocese.*--One who buys the privilege of burying his dead in a cemetery acquires no general right of property, but only a right to use the grounds as a place of interment, and the rules governing a cemetery in force at the time the privilege is acquired measure the extent of the use. Where a rule of the church having charge of the cemetery forbids the burial of non-Catholics therein, the bishop of the diocese and the local priest, who according to the usage of the church were vested with control, had authority and power to restrain a holder of a lot from interring the body of his son who was not in communion with the church at the time of his death, and who committed suicide.(802)

456. *Negroes, Indians.*--The fact that a man is a negro, Indian, or other racial human being, is not good ground to prevent his burial in a cemetery.(803)

457. *Will, Body, Custody.*--Where no disposition of a body has been made by will, the surviving husband, or wife, or next of kin, has the right to the body for the purpose of burial. But the right of the surviving wife or husband, if they were living together at the time of the death of deceased, is paramount to that of the next of kin.(804) A right to the custody of the body of a deceased relative and to decide upon the final place of burial where the deceased is unmarried, is in his next of kin, and this right will be protected by the courts.(805)

458. *Non-Residence, Burial.*--Non-residence does not divest a person of the right to burial with his relatives.(806)

459. *State, Vacate, Equity, Rule.*--The State may require the removal of the bodies and vacate a cemetery without compensation to lot owners in some extraordinary cases of eminent domain or as a health measure.(807) Courts of equity exercise some discretion in cases that do not fall within this rule.(808) But the superintendent of a cemetery has no right to remove a child without the consent of the father who owns the lot.(809)

460. *Consent, Bishop, Removal.*--With the consent of deceased's husband before the funeral, the father of deceased paid for the lot in which his daughter wished to be buried with her parents. Her mother being dissatisfied with the location, the lot was subsequently exchanged for another in the same cemetery; but after preliminary arrangements had been made, the son-in-law applied to a court of equity for a writ restraining the father and the bishop from removing the body. The bishop answered that he was willing to conform to any order of the court. The court held that by acceding to his wife's request and allowing her father to bury her in the first instance, and by standing mute while the arrangements for the removal of the body were being made, the husband had no right thereafter to prevent the removal of his wife's body.(810)

461. *Court, Remove, Consent.*--In a proper case a court may grant a decree to remove the body of a relative from one cemetery to another.(811) Otherwise no one has the right to exhume or remove a body without the consent of those having charge of the cemetery and of those having the right of burial, as consort or the next of kin. In some States the offense is a felony.(812) In Nebraska, at least, those who have the legal right to bury a relative may remove his body from one Catholic cemetery to another without the consent of the bishop.(813)

462. *Crime, Fraud, Exhume, Autopsy.*--In an action on an insurance policy where there is evidence of fraud, as death by poison, a court may order a body exhumed for examination, although the person having the right to control the burial of the body is not a party to the suit.(814) Public officials have the right to disinter a body to ascertain whether a crime has been committed.(815) But without a coroner's inquest or consent of the surviving consort or next of kin, a doctor has no right to perform an autopsy.(816)

463. *Tort, Corpse.*--The general rule is that an action of tort may be maintained by the widow or next of kin for the mutilation of a corpse or even for negligently exposing it to the elements.(817) In a few cases the right has been denied.(818)

464. *Custodian, Burial, Mutilation.*--In the absence of a widow, a son is the lawful custodian of the body of his deceased father for preservation, representation, and burial, and may maintain an action for unlawful mutilation thereof. The sense of outrage and mental suffering resulting directly from the willful mutilation of the body of a parent, is a proper independent element of compensatory damages.(819)

465. *Property in a Corpse, Mummy, Executors.*--The question of property in a corpse has been generally denied. However, in case of a mummy which has become an object of curiosity, the case may be different. Where a testator ordered his body burned and the executor presented a bill for L321 for doing so, the court disallowed it on the ground that when a man is dead his next of kin or executors have the right to dispose of his body; but that as it is not property, a man has no right to bequeath it for a particular purpose.(820) Also, where a man was in jail and died during his imprisonment and the jailer refused to give up the body until the debt was paid, the court held that there was no property in the corpse, and therefore there could be no lien upon it and he must surrender it.(821)

466. *Rights, Duties, Body, Will.*--While there is no property in a dead body so that it may be sold, there are rights and duties out of which may arise tort and criminal actions. The question of the right of a man to dispose of his body by will is not well settled in this country.(822) There are many cases that hold that a person has the right to make a binding testamentary disposition of his own body after death.(823) But on the contrary it has been held that one can not by his will confer any right as to the disposition of his body.(824)

467. *Monument, Fence.*--Giving the right to bury in one's cemetery lot carries with it the right to erect a monument; but it does not carry with it the right to fence the cemetery lot or interfere with other graves therein. Therefore, the monument must be of such size and so located and erected as not to interfere with the rights of others.(825)

468. *Tombstone, Mother-in-Law.*--A husband has the right to remove a tombstone that his mother-in-law put over his wife's grave, and put up one of his own choice instead.(826) The general rule is that vaults and tombstones are personal property and may be removed "in good faith and with care and decency" by the next of kin.(827)

469. *Trees, Authority.*--It is a criminal offense to cut trees in a cemetery without right or authority.(828)

470. *Charitable, Institution, Negligence.*--A Catholic cemetery without capital stock or shares and paying no profits nor dividends, does not come under the head of a charitable institution so as to relieve it from liability for negligence.(829)

471. *Equity, Repair, Injuries.*--A cemetery association may by bill in equity be forced to keep walks and drives in good repair and consequently is liable for injuries resulting from its negligence.(830)

CHAPTER XXXIV.

Domestic Charity Funding of International Operations

The question is whether there are any restrictions on the ability of a U.S. organization to fund international activities.

Fact Assumptions

Suppose that donors of the domestic charity are solicited for donations to be used overseas. Donors are also asked to fund its work in specific nations. Sometimes they are asked to support overseas employees, not all of whom are on the payroll of the domestic charity. Nearly all donations to the domestic charity are made with a designation as to intended use in one form or another. In the event a donor makes a designation which cannot be reasonably accommodated, the donation will either be returned and the donor asked to make a new designation, or the donor will be told his donation will be used elsewhere unless he asks for his money back. Nearly all donations, regardless of how they are designated, will in some part used to compensate international personnel.

Funds are transferred from the central office to the accounts of the various regional offices. Some of the regional directors are on the payroll of the domestic charity. Each time funds are accepted by the regional offices, someone must sign a statement agreeing to honor all fund designations made by U.S. donors. Some of the regional offices have one or more U.S. bank accounts to facilitate funds handling. The regional offices disburse funds to each national charity office which are under them. All national leaders are citizens of the nations in which they work ("nationals"), and are not on the domestic charity payroll. Funds are disbursed by each national charity office for employee support, etc.

Tax Requirements

The law primarily applicable to the use of funds by U.S. organizations overseas is the availability of a charitable deduction for donors of a domestic charity. IRC Sec. 170(c)(2) defines a charitable contribution as a gift to or for the use of a corporation: 1) created or organized in the U.S.; 2) organized and operated exclusively for exempt purposes; 3) in which there is no private increment; and 4) which does not fail to qualify for Sec. 501(c)(3) status by reason of lobbying or political campaigning. If these criteria are not met, a gift to a charity will not be deductible to the donor. See IRC Sec. 170(a)(1).

However, the IRS has taken the position that a U.S. charity cannot be used as a mere conduit for diverting funds to foreign charities. [For purposes of this discussion, what would be considered a foreign charity in the U.S. will be referred to as a "national charity," viewing it from the perspective of the nation in which it exists.] In other words, "to or for the use of" a U.S. charity is interpreted to mean "to and under the control of" a U.S. charity. Where control is lacking, a contribution is not "for the use of" the charity, and a deduction will be denied.

The main concept promoted by the IRS in applicable rulings is that funds contributed to a U.S. charity cannot be earmarked for payment, or subject to an obligation to be paid, to a (foreign) national charity. The circumstances under which deductibility is preserved are discussed below.

CAVEAT: The following discussion applies only to designated funds, that is, donations the donor specifically requests be applied to some international operations, or which the domestic charity is otherwise under an obligation to pass along to another organization. It does not apply to undesignated funds, that is, general donations, employee contributions, administrative charges and other revenues which the domestic charity may choose to apply to international operations. Donations which are not "earmarked" pose no deductibility issue.

Analysis

Under the fact assumptions above, U.S. money leaves the control of the domestic charity at the point where it is used to compensate the services of persons who are not on the payroll of the domestic charity. By definition, these people are not its employees and are not under its legal control. Typically, persons not on the domestic charity payroll are "nationals," although this is not necessarily always the case. Most frequently, once funds leave the control of the regional director's office, they leave control of the domestic charity. The key to this analysis is to realize that when money is used to pay someone not on the domestic payroll, it has been transferred from one organization to another organization. It pays to be very conscious of separate entities. Just because two charities work closely together, even if one was started by the other, it does not mean that they are the same organization. Legal distinctions are real and make a difference!

Donors to the domestic charity will be assured of a charitable contribution deduction for funds which are transferred to an incorporated or otherwise formally organized national charity office separate from the domestic charity only when the following situations exist:

The organized national charity office is controlled by the domestic charity. Tax regulations require the national charity office to be a "mere administrative arm" of the domestic charity. The most clear-cut form of control exists when the national charity is legally a corporate subsidiary of the domestic charity. Tax rulings do not acknowledge that a bare legal affiliate may be considered as a "mere administrative arm" of a domestic charity.

In some countries, a corporate subsidiary relationship may not be possible. Some countries may be hostile toward U.S. control of a national charity, or may oppose the incorporation of charities, etc. In this event, its funding of a national charity must meet the requirements of A.2. or A.3. below.

If the formally organized national charity office is not controlled by the domestic charity, its funding may continue if the following conditions exist:

The national charity is not the exclusive means of charity conducted by the domestic charity in that nation. In other words, the domestic charity must have an independent presence in that nation, apart from the national charity. The primary example given by the IRS when deductibility is preserved is where "a domestic organization conducts a variety of charitable activities in a foreign country." Clearly, this expressly contemplates that the U.S. charity has an independent presence in that nation.

The domestic charity has no obligation to fund the national charity, either by charter, contract, or otherwise. That is, the domestic charity must "maintain at all times full control of the donated funds and discretion as to their use." This does not prohibit the domestic charity donors from designating a national preference, however. So long as the domestic charity has an independent presence in that country, the domestic charity has control over whether to use the funds designated for that nation itself, or pay them over to the national charity.

The domestic charity makes donations to the national charity only out of general or unrestricted funds. In other words, contributions to the domestic charity cannot be earmarked, preferred or designated to be used for the national charity. The domestic charity donors cannot be told their funds will be paid to the national charity, either.

Donations to the national charity serve a charitable purpose of the domestic charity. This means that the domestic charity must regularly review and approve all donations to the national charity. Preferably, this would occur on a project basis. Budgetary review and approval is relevant here.

If the formally organized national charity office is not controlled by the domestic charity, but the domestic charity has no independent presence in that nation, its funding may continue only if the conditions which are described in the accompanying memo, entitled "Relationship of a Domestic Charity Organization to Certain Charitable Foreign Activities" and the attached "Guidelines for Funding Foreign Charities" are satisfied.

In the event a national charity office is not separately organized, it may be a division of a charity formed in another country. If it is a division of the domestic charity, then no problem exists. If it is a division of a charity formed in a different country, then the charity of which it is a part must be treated according to the guidelines in A. above.

In the event the national charity office is not part of a formally organized charity at all, the IRS could either regard the national charity office as an association which can be treated as an organization subject to the guidelines in A. above, or treat payments to nationals as a private inurement, which would seriously jeopardize the exempt status of the domestic charity. For this reason, payments to any national charity office which is not part of a formally organized national charity should be entirely avoided.
Recommendations

The legal structure of the various national charities funded by the domestic charity should be carefully examined. Hopefully, the results of this examination will determine the degree of affiliation between the domestic charity and the various national charity office organizations.

There are a variety of response options:

    Assume legal control of each national charity office organization.

    Modify overseas employee assignments to include the independent presence of U.S. employees in each nation who would work with (but who would not control) the local national charity offices.

    Limit or remove the obligation of regional directors to honor country designations to allow them some true discretion and control over the use of funds.

    Tell U.S. donors that contributions for activities in certain countries are not tax deductible.

    Follow the Guidelines for Funding Foreign Charities, which sets up an accountability mechanism for funding such projects.

    Stop the funding of activities in certain nations.

    One or more of the above responses in combination.

MISCELLANEOUS

472. *Societies, Law.*--Religious societies organized in connection with a church or congregation are in law civil societies and not ecclesiastical corporations, and are governed by the law of the land. Therefore, the law of fraternities fully covers all questions that arise in such societies. The subject is too comprehensive to be treated at any length here.(831)

473. *Society, Bishop.*--A society may expel a member on due notice and a fair trial. The refusal of the bishop to recognize a fraternity organized as a Roman Catholic society, does not prevent the society and its officers from exercising the powers of a religious corporation conferred by law nor prohibit its members from maintaining their religious worship.(832)

474. *Priest, Doorkeeper, Policemen, Arrest.*--A priest who was in charge of a parish and had control of the temporalities consisting of pew-rents, Sunday and other collections, graveyard, church, school, fees, and donations, on account of disorderly behavior of members issued tickets to those to be admitted and ordered a doorkeeper to prevent others from entering the church. A woman without a ticket and talking loudly, endeavored to force her way into the church, although there were several policemen on duty who attempted to stop her. She was arrested and her husband brought suit for false imprisonment. The court held that a clergyman has a right to keep disturbers out of the church and that the doorkeepers have a right to use sufficient force to carry out the orders of the priest; but when a doorkeeper went beyond those orders by causing the arrest of the woman, he was not acting within the apparent scope of his employment and the priest was not liable.(833)

475. *Saloon, Church, License.*--A man owned premises that had been occupied as a saloon from 1894. In 1896 the New York law prohibiting saloons to be licensed within 200 feet of a church, except places where liquor traffic had been carried on prior to that time, was passed. In 1898 a church was built within 200 feet of the saloon in question. After the building of the church, the saloon was vacated for about ten days during a change of saloon keepers, and an action was brought to revoke the license of the new saloon keeper. The court held that the incidental interruption of the business did not bring the place within the prohibition of the law, and that the license could not be revoked.(834)

476. *Y. M. C. A.*--The Y. M. C. A. on account of giving lunches, lectures, and having a gymnasium, for which charges are made, is not a charitable institution so as to be exempt from liability in case of negligence. Property is exempt only when used for exempt purposes exclusively.(835)

477. *Students, Vote, Residence.*--Students at a seminary studying for the priesthood do not thereby lose their residence at their homes and are not entitled to vote where a college is located. The fact that they intend to remain for four years, become clergymen, and then go to wherever they may be called, does not give them the right of residence, and there is no distinction between them and any other students away from home at school.(836) However, a student of full age might become a voter in the college precinct if he has no other fixed domicile.(837)

478. *"My Wife, Anna Jones," Divorce, Insurance.*--A bequest or devise to "my wife, Anna Jones," is not changed by a divorce without some evidence to prove that the testator did not intend his divorced wife to share in his estate, unless the judgment of divorce made a division of the property. The same is true of a policy of insurance or benefit certificate. However, there are exceptions that weaken the rule and make its application in some States uncertain.(838)

479. *Bells, Sick, Injunction.*--On the complaint of an injured person, a court will issue an injunction restraining the ringing of church, convent, or other bells, at unusual hours or when their noise is injurious to the sick, or when their vibration affects other premises. As the law of nuisances applies in such cases, an exact statement of when the court should issue the injunction or whether the injunction should be temporary or perpetual, can not be given; but when the personal or property rights of others are affected, an injunction may be granted. The fact that the bells are chimes or part of a clock does not change the rule.(839)

480. *Marriage, Impediments, Recording.*--Legal marriage may be contracted only between unmarried persons not related within the prohibited degrees of consanguinity or affinity, of lawful age and sufficient mental and physical capacity. Statutes vary greatly. In some States affinity is not considered a legal objection and first cousins may marry; in others, both are prohibited and other limitations of relationship, race, and color are fixed, and registration of the clergymen and licenses to wed are required. Also, the clergyman must report the marriage promptly to the proper office. Fines, penalties, and imprisonment are usually provided for violating the law. Informal marriages may or may not be voidable or void.(840)

481. *Charivari, Wedding Pranks*.--Charivari, assaults, and disorderly conduct are unlawful at all times, and can not be justified by custom.(841) A newly wedded man who was serenaded (charivaried) by his neighbors by firing guns, blowing horns, beating pans, rattling horse-fiddles, etc., after ordering the rioters off fired into the crowd and wounded one of them. On trial for assault with intent to kill, the groom was acquitted. Shooting might not be justifiable in cases where less potent agencies, such as a horsewhip or dogs, are sufficient, or where the immediate protection of person or property does not call for it. The law should be invoked when no exigency for force exists.(842)

482. *Infallibility of Courts*.--When a question of law at issue in a case is duly presented to a supreme court which is the court of last resort, its decision thereon becomes "the law of the case" and is thereafter binding upon the court itself and all the courts inferior to it; and no matter how often that identical case may come before the court on subsequent appeals, the questions already decided therein will not be reconsidered. It is interesting to compare this principle of our courts with Papal infallibility.(843) Courts do not always adhere to the rule. (844)

483. *Money Stolen, Bailed or Loaned, Insolvency, Gifts*.--Property stolen by A. or left with him as bailee to be returned in specie, can not be given away by him for charity. Also, when a man is insolvent he has no right to give away any of his property.(845) That has been the rule of law since Coke laid down the maxim: "A man must be just before he is generous." One is insolvent when his debts exceed the value of his unexempt property.(846) When an insolvent debtor makes a gift, a creditor may sue and recover from the donee; or in a proper case the creditor may force the debtor into bankruptcy to recover the gift.(847) The want of knowledge or good faith of the donee is immaterial and no defense to an action to recover the property.(848)

Chapter XXXV

Tax Provisions Affecting Clergy

A. COMPENSATION. The compensation of ministers is subject to several significant exceptions and exclusions compared not only to non-church employees, but also to other church employees.

1. For §403(b) plan purposes, ministers get special breaks in computing contribution limits compared to other plan participants.

2. For church plan purposes, ministers who are self-employed may be covered the same as regular employees. Even ministers who are employed by a non-church organization may nonetheless sometimes participate in a church plan through their ecclesiastical structure.

3. Wages earned by a minister performing services "in the exercise of his ministry" are excluded from withholding requirements. §3401(a)(9).

4. Ministers and other church employees have special exemptions from FUTA (unemployment tax). §3309(b)(1) & (2).

5. Be aware that some ministers, in certain religious traditions, view themselves as self-employed and not as employees, i.e., their compensation is reported on Form 1099 rather than Form W-2. Generally, this position cannot be properly sustained. However, even here there are exceptions and recent cases occasionally still conclude the minister is truly self-employed. But this is the exception, not the rule.

B. SOCIAL SECURITY TAXES.

1. Although regular church employees have been subject to FICA since 1984, FICA is inapplicable (per IRC §3121(b)(8)) to:

    a. a minister "performing services in the exercise of his ministry" [a term of art], or a member of a religious order performing services in the exercise of duties required by the order; and

    b. employees of a church or church-controlled organization if: (a) the organization is opposed for religious reasons to the payment of FICA taxes; and (b) the services are not performed in an unrelated trade or business. See also §3121(w).

2. What this means is that ministers are treated, for social security purposes, as though they were self-employed. [CAVEAT: This does not mean a minister is actually self-employed, either for other federal tax purposes (ministers do not file Schedule C just because they are covered by SECA) or for any state law purpose. But it is confusing - especially to clients.]

    a. Thus, ministers come under the provisions of SECA (the self-employment tax). See IRC §1402(a)(8). SECA must be paid with respect to a pre-retirement housing allowance, but not with respect to a post-retirement housing allowance or a post-retirement benefit received from a church plan.

    b. Of course, there are special rules for certain church employee income. See §1402(j). And the regulations under §1402 are absolutely crucial.

    c. For ministers, all 403(b) contributions within the exclusion allowance are not subject to SECA, whether made by the employer or the minister.   For other church employees, salary deferrals are subject to FICA, but employer contributions are not subject to FICA. For all employees, 403(b) contributions in excess of the exclusion allowance are subject to SECA or FICA. Now isn't that simple?

3. Opting out of social security. Additionally, ministers and members of religious orders may 'opt out' of social security altogether under §1402(e)(1) if they are conscientiously or religiously opposed to the acceptance of public insurance payments. This is a fairly common practice among missionary organizations or any 'support-raising' ecclesiastical organization.

C. MINISTERS' PARSONAGE (RENTAL HOUSING) ALLOWANCE.

1. Ministers, but not other church employees and not members of a religious order, may exclude from income the housing allowance permitted by IRC §107. It is quite common for ministers to take up to 50% of their total compensation in the form of a housing allowance.

2. There are a host of rules applicable to housing allowances, most of which relate to the definition of what constitutes "services performed in the exercise of ministry" and can be found in the Regs. under §1402. The amount excludible from income is the least of the following three amounts:

    a. The actual expenses incurred by the minister for qualified housing purposes;

    b. The amount declared in advance of payment by the minister's employer as constituting a housing allowance; and

    c. The fair rental value of the minister's home, and for years after 2001, this amount includes the fair rental value of furnishings and appurtenances such as a garage, plus the cost of utilities.

3. Some key points to remember:

    a. Exclusion from income as a housing allowance is not something which the minister can decide, or accomplish, on their own. Merely being a minister does not qualify someone for taking the exclusion. Unless the employer has formally adopted a housing allowance for the minister, it does not exist.

    b. Whenever a minister is employed by any organization unrelated to his or her ordaining body, a "letter of assignment" from the ordaining body which meets certain prerequisites is required to sustain the income exclusion.

    c. Not all compensation received by the minister qualifies for the income exclusion. Only compensation paid for services performed in the exercise of ministry qualify. Generally, this is not a problem for clergy who perform administrative tasks for a church or who teach at a religious seminary, but are more problematic for chaplains and other ministers employed by a secular employer.
    ci.

Chapter XXXVI

Relationship of a Domestic Charity Organization to Certain Charitable Foreign Activities

Can a domestic charity, as an IRC Section 501(c)(3) tax-exempt organization, fund the activities of national charity offices and other foreign projects in such a way that its exempt status is not jeopardized and donor deductibility is fully preserved, without the domestic charity exercising legal control over such organizations or projects? The short answer is "yes."

Fact Assumptions

The domestic charity is a Section 501(c)(3) charitable organization that has significant foreign involvement in charitable activities. Currently, the domestic charity donors are solicited for donations to be used in foreign locations and at times are asked to support foreign staff, some of whom are on the domestic charity payroll and some of whom are not. Most donations are made with a designation of intended use (name of country) and most such donations are used by the domestic charity to compensate international personnel. Funds are transferred from the central office to accounts of various regional offices which then disburse funds to each national charity office for staff support and other purposes.

Summary

Although exempt status of a Section 501(c)(3) organization is not jeopardized by the transmission of a portion or all of its funds to assist foreign charitable activities, the IRS has disallowed charitable deductions where domestic exempt organizations do not exercise adequate discretion and control over grants made to foreign organizations. The IRS has recognized periodic reporting requirements and other monitoring of foreign grantees as elements of requisite discretion and control. The domestic charity can adopt and apply foreign funding guidelines which have been prepared to comply with these requirements. Neither legal control of the foreign organization nor an independent presence by the domestic charity in the foreign country is required to assure charitable deductions to donors. The domestic charity may even accept designated contributions for foreign charitable activities as long as the domestic charity board follows certain guidelines.

The IRS looks at four criteria in foreign funding situations to determine if contributions to the domestic charity are deductible: (1) the specific project to be carried out by the foreign organization must fulfill the exempt purposes of the domestic charity; (2) the board of the domestic charity must review and approve the specific foreign project; (3) the domestic charity must maintain full control and discretion over the donated funds; and (4) the domestic charity must not be a passive conduit of earmarked funds. The test is whether the domestic charity is the real recipient of the contributions, and demonstrates bona fide control and discretion over how the funds are disbursed by it to foreign projects. The IRS has pointed to such factors as the following to indicate that these requirements are met:

The domestic charity legally controls and operates the foreign organization to which it channels funds. (Satisfaction of this factor alone would be sufficient without any others to justify deductibility of U.S. Donations.)

The domestic charity's board reviews and approves the project in the foreign country for which funds will be spent.

The domestic charity monitors and oversees the foreign project through appropriate field review.

The domestic charity retains full control of the donated funds and exercises discretion as to their use (even to the point of retaining the right to terminate further funding and withdraw unspent funds at any time) so as to ensure they will be used to carry out the domestic charity's function and purposes.

The domestic charity receives periodic accounting of all funds to assure compliance these unique discretionary duties.

The Funding of Foreign Charitable Organizations

The IRS will disallow a tax deduction for contributions to domestic charities if the domestic charities are "mere conduits" of funds to foreign organizations. To determine whether the charity is more than a mere conduit, the IRS looks carefully at whether the domestic charity exercises sufficient "discretion and control" over contributed funds. The issue of the required control by a Section 501(c)(3) organization over charitable projects in foreign countries sufficient to protect tax deductibility is not addressed in the Internal Revenue Code or its regulations. The IRS, however, has addressed this issue in individual revenue rulings regarding charitable gifts channeled to foreign countries. It has developed a set of guidelines to determine whether a gift to a U.S. charity is tax deductible when it is ultimately used to further charitable purposes in another country. Analysis and application of these guidelines will enable a domestic charity to channel a portion or all of its charitable funds to foreign charitable entities or projects while still preserving for its U.S. donors full tax deductibility treatment.

Contributions to Foreign Charities are not Deductible. The IRS and courts have consistently held that contributions to foreign charities are not deductible on U.S. tax returns. See e.g., M. ErSelcuk, 30 T.C. 962 (1958); L.K. Herter, 20 T.C.M. 78; R. Hess, 30 T.C.M. 1043. Even contributions made to a bi national charitable foundation which was created by executive agreement between the U.S. and a foreign country, financed by property contributed equally by the two countries and whose assets were to be equally divided between the U.S. and the foreign country, were not deductible. Rev. Rul. 76-195, 1976-1 C.B. 61. The question then becomes whether a charitable deduction would be allowed if made to a bona fide tax-exempt entity in the U.S. which then expends its funds for activities in a foreign country.

Contributions to U.S. Charities which Operate in a Foreign Country are Deductible. A domestic charity that conducts a part or all of its charitable activities in a foreign country is not precluded under Section 501(c)(3) from exemption. Rev. Rul. 71-460, 1971-2 C.B. 231. The IRS permits deductibility for contributions to Section 501(c)(3) organizations created in the U.S. but which operate to some extent in foreign countries as long as two requirements are met:

The domestic charity must qualify under Section 170(c)(2)(A) of the Internal Revenue Code which requires an exempt organization to be created or organized in the U.S. or in its possessions. Rev. Rul. 63-252, 1963-2 C.B. 101.

The domestic charity must be organized and operated exclusively for one of the purposes stated in Section 170(c)(2)(B) of the Code, such as religious, charitable, scientific, literary, or educational and it must also meet the other requirements of Section 170(c)(2) of the Code (no private inurement, no impermissible political activity, etc.).

The domestic charity could operate under this model and assure full donor deductibility provided all foreign activities were conducted under its full organizational control, either under the auspices of its domestic entity or through a subsidiary foreign entity. However, other alternatives will also be examined.

Contributions to U.S. Charities which in Turn Make Grants to Foreign Charities are Deductible in Limited Circumstances. Under this alternative, the domestic charity could fund foreign charity through grants to compatible but separate organizations. There are several variations:

A deduction will be disallowed for contributions made to a U.S. tax-exempt organization which turns over 100 percent of its charitable contributions to a foreign charity. Rev. Rul. 63-252, 1963-2, C.B. 10. The IRS reasons that the requirements of Section 170(c)(2)(A) described above would be "nullified if contributions inevitably committed to go to a foreign organization were held to be deductible solely because, in the course of the transmittal to the foreign organization, they came to rest momentarily in a qualifying domestic organization. In such cases, the domestic organization is only nominally the donee; the real donee is the ultimate foreign recipient." Rev. Rul. 63-252, 1963-2 C.B. 101. This is what is called the "passive conduit" model.

Contributions to a domestic charity that are solicited for a specific project of a foreign charitable organization are deductible where the domestic charity has reviewed and approved the project as being in furtherance of its own exempt purposes and has control and discretion as to the use of the contributions. Rev. Rul. 66-79, 1966-1 C.b. 48, amplifying Rev. Rul. 63-252. This is the category under which most of the domestic charity's gifts and grants to a foreign charitable organization would occur.

This underscores the importance of the budgetary process for maintaining the requisite control. In addition to listing the directors' exclusive authority to make grants, their responsibility to review specific projects in advance of funding, and absolute discretion to refuse to render financial assistance and refuse earmarked or designated funds, the IRS noted approvingly that the directors required the grantees to "furnish a periodic accounting to show that the funds were expended for the purposes which were approved by the board of directors," and that the board retained at all times the right to withdraw approval of the grant. Rev. Rule 66-79, 1966-1 C.B. 48.

It is important to note that the IRS has not established any one or several of these criteria as essential for proving that a domestic charity has exercised sufficient discretion and control. Neither has the IRS defined how much monitoring would be sufficient to establish the requisite control. Given that IRS rulings also cite the ability of a board to cease funding if exempt purposes are not being pursued as expected, it is desirable that a domestic charity require sufficient monitoring to determine whether funding should be continued. It is recommended that periodic accounting and monitoring be undertaken with each grant in excess of a minimal amount (e.g., $5,000) to ensure "full control of the donated funds, and discretion as to their use." Rev. Rul 66-79.

Whether the proper amount of control has been exercised is determined by the IRS on a case-by-case basis as shown in the following rulings.

Where a domestic charity received contributions in furtherance of its exempt purposes and made grants from its general funds to various foreign organizations to support restoration work in the foreign country, a deduction for the contributions was allowed. The IRS found the proper control was exercised since: 1) the trustee reviewed and approved the project and contributions were solicited specifically for this project and receipted through a special committee set up for this purpose; and 2) the domestic charity retained full control of the donations for this project and discretion as to their particular use as evidenced by its reservation of the right to designate the specific renovation to be made, to receive periodic accounting of all funds, and to withdraw its support at any time at its discretion. PLR No. 8408062.

Similarly, where a domestic charity received contributions in keeping with its educational purpose for the restoration and rehabilitation of the birthplace of "A" in a foreign country, the IRS allowed a deduction for the contributions. The domestic charity demonstrated its control by: 1) board review and approval of the project; 2) the establishment of a special committee to assist in the management of contributions made to the domestic charity for the project; 3) the establishment of a separate bank account; 4) separate financial and administrative records of such contributions; 5) supervision of the expenditure of the funds in a manner consistent with the charter and policies of the domestic charity; 6) retention of absolute discretion to withdraw the special funds for use toward other exempt purposes of the domestic charity; and 7) advising potential contributors of this discretionary duty. PLR No. 8346038.

In another private letter ruling, the IRS held contributions to a domestic charity for use by a foreign organization deductible when the following limitations were present: 1) no member of the domestic charity's board of directors was a member of the foreign organization's board; 2) the domestic charity's decisions as to the disposition of contributions were wholly independent of the foreign organization; 3) the domestic charity's board reviewed and approved each specific project; and 4) the domestic charity monitored the use of funds given to the foreign organization. PLR No. 8340031.

Rev. Rul. 66-79, 1966-1 C.B. 48 again illustrates the IRS's willingness to allow a deduction for contributions made to the domestic charity for use by a foreign organization so long as certain safeguards are present. Here, the domestic charity had been organized with a goal of raising funds for specific projects, such as science research projects, to be carried out by the foreign organization. Therefore, the bylaws stipulated the following: 1) the board of directors has exclusive control over the making of grants or other financial assistance; 2) the board has power to make grants in furtherance of the exempt purposes of the domestic charity; 3) the board reviews, approves and authorizes each grant; 4) there must be a periodic accounting to show the funds are being used appropriately; 5) the board has absolute discretion to refuse to make any such grants and can at any time withdraw approval of a grant; 6) all of the pertinent facts shall be made available to any contributor upon request. The IRS identified in this revenue ruling the test as to whether the domestic organization has "full control of the donated funds, and discretion as to their use, so as to ensure that they will be used to carry out [the domestic charity's] functions and purposes." In this instance because the bylaws outlined the conditions of review, control and discretion, the IRS permitted the deduction of charitable contributions to that domestic charity.

Revenue Ruling 66-79 described above amplified Rev. Rul. 63-252, 1963-2 C.B. 101, in which the IRS first outlined its requirements for the allowance of contributions made to a domestic charity for use by a foreign entity. In Rev. Rul. 63-252, the IRS outlined five examples to illustrate its requirements:

    A foreign organization desiring to solicit funds causes a domestic charity to be formed and proposes the domestic charity conduct a fund raising drive, pay the administrative expenses from collected funds and remit the balance to the foreign organization.

    U.S. citizens desiring to assist a foreign organization's work from a domestic charity whose charter provides it will receive contributions and send them periodically to the foreign organization.

    A foreign organization agrees with the domestic charity that the domestic charity will conduct a fund raising campaign on its behalf and remit to it the net funds raised.

    A domestic charity conducts a variety of charitable activities in a foreign country. When its purposes can be furthered by granting funds to charitable groups organized in the foreign country, the domestic charity makes grants for purposes it has reviewed and approved. The domestic charity makes grants from its general funds. No special fund is raised by solicitation on behalf of particular foreign organizations.

    A domestic charity conducting charitable work in a foreign country formed a subsidiary there to facilitate its operations. The domestic charity controls every facet of its operations and the foreign organization is merely an administrative arm of the domestic charity. The domestic charity solicits funds specifically for its foreign work.

Rev. Rul. 63-252 held that contributions to organizations described in the first three examples were not deductible and that contributions to the organizations described in examples four and five were deductible. In the last two examples, the three main characteristics of furtherance of exempt purposes, review and approval, and control and discretion are present. However, the IRS also noted that these contributions were either not specifically earmarked or where they were, the true recipient was found to be the domestic charity.

Conclusion. The domestic charity may make grants or transmit funds to a charitable organization in a foreign country without jeopardizing its tax-exempt status. However, the IRS regulates such transactions not through its tax exemption authority under IRC Section 501(c)(3) but rather through its charitable deduction authority under IRC Section 170. By placing requirements on the transfer of funds from a domestic charity to a foreign organization which are necessary to secure deductibility of contributions, the IRS effectively regulates the charitable activities of U.S. exempt organizations in foreign countries. As long as the domestic charity follows the guidelines described herein, it may properly devote some or all of its funds to projects of foreign charitable organizations without jeopardizing the charitable tax deduction of its U.S. donors.

Adoption of the attached Guidelines and pre-approval of specific projects by the domestic charity Board of Directors will demonstrate that the domestic charity acts independently of its grantees in determining how funds will be expended. Periodic accounting as required by the Guidelines together with receipt and review of reports from grantees by a subcommittee of the board or officers of the domestic charity also provides evidence of requisite discretion and control.

Independent Presence of the Domestic Charity Not Required. One proposed solution to the problem of funding national charity offices is to place the domestic charity staff in countries where all of the domestic charity's operations are currently performed by resident nationals. However, requisite expenditure control does not require making this type of oversight. The domestic charity agents or employees could make periodic visits or the domestic charity could delegate to a responsible foreign agent the oversight responsibility to observe and report on the work of the national charity offices.

Donor Designation Not Necessarily Forbidden. While it is true that the donor designations must not be allowed to short circuit proper board oversight and control, such designations are wholly proper if the board has previously evaluated, selected and presented through informed decision making, a buffet of foreign projects for donor selection. Additionally, donor designations for projects outside the current buffet of board approved projects may be considered for funding provided the board adheres to its "control and discretion" guidelines.

Legal Control by the Domestic Charity Over National Charity Offices is Not Required. Finally, it is not necessary for the domestic charity to exercise legal control over the national charity offices. Proper expenditure control as proposed in the Guidelines is sufficient to meet IRS requirements. Often, there is concern that due to the nature of the domestic charity goals and philosophy, the decentralized emphasis of indigenous national charity offices would be threatened by the domestic charity having to exert legal control over the entities to meet IRS requirements for donor deductibility of contributions. Many of the field offices in foreign countries incorporate in the foreign country out of their own initiative, not a the domestic charity direction or mandate.

As explained above, legal control is not required. In fact, the stringent expenditure control required of private foundations is not required for public foundations. As long as the domestic charity follows the attached Guidelines regarding proper discretion and control, the domestic charity may offer donors full tax deductibility without exercising legal control of its national charity offices.

The Funding of Foreign Staff

The domestic charity receives donations for foreign staff, some of whom are on the payroll of the domestic charity and some of whom are not. Resident nationals are typically on the payroll of the national charity office and not the domestic charity. The question arises whether the domestic charity may ensure the charitable deduction for a donor who designates a contribution for a specific individual who is on foreign staff of a national charity office or for a the domestic charity employee working in a particular foreign country.

Funding of Resident Nationals. As explained above, the domestic charity can make a grant to a national charity office that would cover a number of budgetary items, including salaries. As long as the requisite discretion and control is maintained, the domestic charity can receive designated contributions for pre-budgeted, board approved expenditures including resident nationals' salary requirements and fund those through grants to the national charity office.

Funding of the Domestic Charity Staff in Foreign Countries. The domestic charity employees who are operating in a foreign country are essentially missionaries of the domestic charity to that foreign country. The ability of the domestic charity to accept designated contributions for these missionaries depends on the domestic charity's exercise of discretion and control over donated funds. The domestic charity generally may honor designated contributions for particular staff as long as the domestic charity retains full discretion over the ultimate expenditure or use of those contributions. This can be accomplished by following the Guidelines (i.e., board preapproval of budgets, including salaries, and of the activities and mission statement of each approved foreign staff, together with regular monitoring of financial, comparing actual with budget figures, program review, etc.).

Conclusion

The domestic charity is not required by current IRS Code, regulations or case law to exercise legal control over national charity offices, have an independent presence in countries where national charity offices exist, or prohibit designated contributions for these foreign charities to ensure donor deductibility of contributions for foreign charitable activities. The domestic charity is required to exercise requisite discretion and control as outlined above. Generally, the IRS will conclude that boards of directors have exercised sufficient control and discretion over foreign grants and projects if at least 1-4 of the following board practices are implemented:

Board review, approval and authorization of each grant proposal to ensure compliance with the charter and policies of the domestic charity.

Adequate periodic reporting requirements to demonstrate satisfaction of agreed standards of performance and accountability.

Board retention of full control and absolute discretion over use of all donated funds, including the right to discontinue further funding of foreign projects that fail to satisfy standards of performance or accountability.

Board disclosure to contributors that it, and not the foreign organization, has complete discretion over the use of funds contributed.

Special board committee to monitor and oversee foreign projects.

Maintenance of special bank account and separate financial records of contributions for foreign projects.

These practices have been incorporated into Guidelines for Funding Foreign Charities which the domestic charity Board should review, adopt and implement.

Again I would like to thank all of the contributors especially Thompson and Thompson Law Firm in Livona, MI for providing the information to compile this book. If you have any questions concerning Law and your Church, call them or another attorney before the situation gets out of hand. Remember what Benjamin Franklin said :

"An ounce of prevention is worth a pound of cure".

FOOTNOTES
1 U. S. Constitution, Amendments, art. i, art. xiv, sec. 1.
2 Lives of the Popes, Montor, vol. i, p. 94; Life of Leo XIII, "Philippine Question."
3 The Science of Jurisprudence, Taylor, p. 506; Historical Jurisprudence, Lee, p. 328.
4 Ancient Egypt, Rawlinson, vol. i, p. 323.
5 Historical Jurisprudence, Lee, pp. 98, 164, 274; History of England, Lingard, vol. i, c. vii; The Science of Jurisprudence, Taylor, p. 506.
6 Historical Jurisprudence, Lee, p. 257.
7 Historical Jurisprudence, Lee, p. 271.
8 The Beginnings of Christianity, Shahan, 90.
9 Elements of Ecclesiastical Law, Smith.
10 Historical Jurisprudence, Lee, p. 387; Justinian, Sandar, p. 21.
11 The Beginnings of Christianity, Shahan.
12 Universal Church History, Alzog.
13 Law Dictionary, Bouvier, "Benefit of Clergy," "Canon Law"; Blackstone, vol. i,

p. 460, vol. iii, p. 61.
14 Blackstone, vol. i, p. 461.
15 Justinian, Sandar, p. 21; Cyc, vol. viii, p. 366, vol. xiv, p. 1228; Eq. Jurisprudence, Pomeroy, vol. i, p. 1; The Science of Jurisprudence, Taylor, p. 255 et seq; Blackstone, vol. i, pp. 18-20, 63; Kent, vol. i, p. 10; English Constitution, Creasy.
16 Blackstone, vol. i, p. 82, vol. iv, c. 33; The Science of Jurisprudence, Taylor, p. 337; Conflict of Laws, Wharton, sec. 172.
17 The American Cyclopedia, "Bologna."
18 The Science of Jurisprudence, Taylor, p. 238.
19 Blackstone, vol. i, pp. 18-20, 79, vol. iv, c. 33.
20 Commentaries, Kent, vol. i, c. xi, pp. 342, 473, 515, 525-544, vol. ii, p. 27; Origin and Nature of the Constitution and Government of U. S., U. S. Sup. Ct. Reps., 9 L. Ed., 873.
21 Commentaries, Kent, vol. i, p. 472; Blackstone, vol. i, p. 107.
22 Commentaries, Kent, vol. ii, pp. 35-37; Conflict of Laws, Wharton (3rd ed.), vol. ii, pp. 1327-8.
23 Law of Fraternities, Scanlan, ch. xxiv; Conflict of Laws, Wharton, sec. 109; Baxter v. McDonald, 155 N. Y., 83; 49 N. E., 667; Morris v. Dart, 67 S. C, 338; 45 S. E., 753; 100 Am. St. R., 734; Terrett v. Taylor, 13 U. S., 43; 3 L. Ed., 650.
24 Weld v. May, 9 Cushing, Mass., 181.
25 Martin v. State, 65 Tenn., 234.
26 A Manual of Catholic Theology, Wilhelm and Scannell, p. xvii, et seq.
27 A Catholic Dictionary, Addis and Arnold, "Dogma."
28 In re St. Louis Inst. of Christian Science, 27 Mo. App., 633.
29 Hale v. Everett, 53 N. H., 9.
30 State v. Trustees, 7 Ohio St., 58.
31 Kniskern v. Lutheran Church, 1 Sandford, N. Y., Ch. 439.
32 State v. Hallock, 16 Nev., 373.
33 Stephenson v. Hanyon, 7 Dist. Ct. Rep. Pa., 585.
34 State v. Board, 134 Mo., 296; 35 S. W., 617.
35 Synod v. State, 2 S. Dak., 366; 50 N. W., 632; 14 L. R. A., 418.
36 Stebbins v. Jennings, 10 Pick., Mass., 172.
37 State v. District Board, 76 Wis., 177; 44 N. W., 967; 20 Am. St. Rep., 41; 7 L. R. A., 330.
38 Hackett v. Brooksville, 27 Ky. L., 1021; 87 N. W., 792; 69 L. R. A., 592.
39 State v. Board, 134 Mo., 296; 35 S. W., 617; 56 Am. St. Rep., 503.
40 County v. Industrial School, 125 Ill., 540; 18 N. E., 183; 1 L. R. A., 437; 8 Am. St. Rep., 386.
41 "Wis. Industrial School for Girls," Wisconsin Blue Book. Session Laws of Wis., 1907, p. 1416 (index to Acts). Wis. Industrial School for Girls v. Clark Co., 103 Wis., 651; 79 N. W., 422.
42 O'Connor v. Hendrick, 184 N. Y., 421; 77 N. E., 612.
43 Hysong v. Gallitzen, 164 Pa., 629; 30 At., 482; 44 Am. St. Rep., 623; 26 L. R. A., 203; Dorner v. School Dist., 118 N. W., 353 (Nov. 27, 1908). A good resume of the subject is given in a footnote in 105 Am. St. R., 151.
44 Stafford v. State, 45 So., 673. A Protestant Dictionary, Wright & Neil, and

Webster's Dictionary, "Worship." A Catholic Dictionary, Addis and Arnold, "Latria."
45 Gass's App., 73 Pa., 46; 13 Am. Rep., 726; State v. Norris, 59 N. H., 536.
46 St. Joseph's Church v. Assessors, 12 R. I., 19; 34 Am. R., 597; Gerke v. Purcell, 25 Ohio, 229; Am. & Eng. Ency. of L., "Worship."
47 Ante, 28; Post, 346.
48 Catholic Catechism.
49 Sherman v. Baker, 20 R. I., 446; 40 At., 11; 40 L. R. A., 717.
50 Webster v. Surghow, 69 N. H., 380; 45 At., 139; 48 L. R. A., 100.
51 Coleman v. O'Leary, 114 Ky., 388; 70 S. W., 1068.
52 McEntee v. Bonacum, 66 Neb., 651; 92 N. W., 633.
53 American and English Encyclopedia of Law, "Parishoner."
54 Ibid., "Minister"; 7 Cyc, 189, "Clergy."
55 Ibid.
56 Ibid.
57 Davies v. Beason, 133 U. S., 333; 33 L. Ed., 637.
58 Simpson v. Welcome, 72 Me., 496.
59 Board v. Minor, 23 Ohio St., 250.
60 Baxter v. Langley, 38 L. J., M. C., 1.
61 Art. vi.
62 Ex parte Garland, 4 Wallace, 333; 18 L. Ed., 366.
63 Church of Latter-Day Saints v. U. S., 136 U. S., 1; 34 L. Ed., 478; 140 U. S., 665; 35 L. Ed., 592.
64 Reynolds v. United States, 8 Otto, 145; 25 L. Ed., 244.
65 Church of Latter-Day Saints v. U. S., 136 U. S., 1; 34 L. Ed., 478; 140 U. S., 665; 35 L. Ed., 592.
66 Davis v. Beason, 133 U. S., 333; 33 L. Ed., 637.
67 Fenelon v. Girard, 2 Howard, 127; 11 L. Ed., 205.
68 State v. Marble, 72 Ohio St., 21; 73 N. E., 1063; State v. Chenoweth, 163 Ind., 94; 71 N. E., 197; People v. Reetz, 127 Mich, 87; 86 N. W., 396; 59 Cen. L. J., 202; 68 L. R. A., 432.
69 Thaxter v. Jones, 4 Mass., 570.
70 Hale v. Everett, 53 N. H., 9.
71 Federal and State Constitutions, Stimson.
72 Bradford v. Roberts, 175 U. S., 291; 44 L. Ed., 168; 20 Sup. Ct. R., 121; Municipality of Ponce v. The Roman Catholic Apostolic Church, 28 Sup. Ct. R., 737 (1908).
73 Terrett v. Taylor, 9 Cranch, 43; 3 L. Ed., 650; Municipality, etc., v. Church, 28 Sup. Ct. R., 737.
74 Millard v. Board, 19 Ill., 48; Dorner v. Dist., 118 N. W., 353.
75 Ashby v. Wellington, 25 Mass., 524.
76 Federal and State Constitutions, Stimson, p. 139; Hale v. Everett, 53 N. H., 9.
77 State v. Trustees, 11 Ohio, 24.
78 First v. Leach, 35 Vt., 108.
79 Federal and State Constitutions, Stimson, p. 139.
80 State v. District, 76 Wis., 177; 44 N. W., 967; 20 Am. St. R., 41; 7 L. R. A., 330.

81 Church v. Bullock, 100 S. W. (Tex.), 1025; Millard v. Board, 121 Ill., 297; 10 N. E., 669; Hackett v. Brooksville, 27 Ky. L., 1021; 87 S. W., 792; 69 L. R. A., 592; 61 C. L. J., 49.
82 Church v. Bullock, 100 S. W., 1025.
83 Moore v. Monroe, 64 Ia., 367; 20 N. W., 475; 66 L. R. A., 166; 52 Am. R., 444; Pfeiffer v. Board, 118 Mich., 560; 77 N. W., 250; 42 L. R. A., 536.
84 Hysong v. Gallitzin Borough School, 164 Pa. St., 629; 30 At., 482; 26 L. R. A., 203; Dorner v. School District, 118 N. W., Wis., 353 (Nov. 27, 1908).
85 O'Connor v. Hendricks, 96 N. Y. S., 161.
86 Ch. 723, L. 1895.
87 West v. Otteson, 80 Wis., 62; 49 N. W., 24; Ferraria v. Vasconcellos, 23 Ill., 456; 31 Ill., 25.
88 Gitzhoffen v. Sisters, 88 Pac., 691; 32 Utah, 46; Trustees v. B. P. O. E., 122 Wis., 452; 100 N. W., 837.
89 Hermits v. County, 7 Pa. L. J., 124.
90 Trustees v. Manning, 72 Md., 116; 19 At., 599.
91 In re Van Horn, 18 R. I., 389.
92 Wardens v. Blanc, 8 Rob, La., 51.
93 Rutherford v. Hill, 22 Or., 218; 29 Pac., 546; 17 L. R. A., 549; 56 Cen. L. J., 221; Wechselberg v. Flour, 64 F., 90.
94 Jewett v. Thames Bank, 16 Conn., 511.
95 Jeffts v. York, 10 Cushing, 392.
96 Allen v. M. E. Church, 127 Ia., 96; 102 N. W., 808; 69 L. R. A., 255; Sawyer v. Methodist, 18 Vt., 405.
97 Wise v. Perpetual Trustees, House of Lords, 57 C. L. J., 104.
98 Sheehy v. Blake, 77 Wis., 394; 46 N. W., 537; 69 L. R. A., 255.
99 Clark v. O'Rourke, 111 Mich., 108; 69 N. W., 147.
100 Bradford v. Cary, 5 Me., 339; Lynch v. Pfeiffer, 110 N. Y., 33; 17 N. E., 402; In re St. Luke's, 17 Philadelphia, 261.
101 Addison v. Brock, 3 Me., 243.
102 Stebbins v. Jennings, 10 Pickering, 172.
103 Municipality of Ponce v. Roman Catholic Church, 28 Sup. Ct. R., 737; 6 Cyc, 915.
104 Ferraria v. Vasconcellos, 31 Ill., 25; Mason v. Muncaster, 9 Wheaton, 468; 6 L. Ed., 131.
105 Wheaton v. Gates, 18 N. Y., 395.
106 South v. Yates, 1 Hoff. N. Y., 142; Miller v. Chittendon, 42 Ia., 252; Newmarket v. Smart, 45 N. H., 87; Evangelical Appeal, 35 Pa. St., 316.
107 Congregational Society v. Swan, 2 Vt., 222.
108 Horton v. Baptist Church, 34 Vt., 309.
109 Associated Reform Church v. Theological Seminary, 4 N. J. Eq., 77.
110 Taylor v. Edison, 4 Cushing, 522.
111 Laws of 1895, ch. 723; Religious Corporations, Cummings and Gilbert.
112 Heiss v. Vosburg, 59 Wis., 532; 18 N. W., 463.
113 Tartar v. Gibbs, 24 Md., 323.
114 Christian C. v. C., 219 Ill., 503; 76 N. E., 703.
115 Jackson v. Legate, 9 Wendell, N. Y., 377.

116 10 Cyc, 235-244.
117 Atty-Gen. v. Dutch, 36 N. Y., 452.
118 Methodist v. Pickett, 23 Barber, 436.
119 Sutton v. Cole, 8 Mass., 96.
120 Miller v. English, 21 N. J. L., 317.
121 Enos v. Church, 187 Mass., 40; 72 N. E., 253.
122 Baptist v. Wetherell, 3 Paige, N. Y., 296; In re Williams, 105 N. Y. S., 1105; Contra: First R. P. Ch. v. Bowden, 10 Abb., N. C., 1.
123 Bellports v. Tooker, 29 Barber, N. Y., 256.
124 Sutter v. First, 42 Pa. St., 503.
125 Atwater v. Woodbridge, 6 Conn., 223.
126 Wardens v. Hall, 22 Conn., 125.
127 Beach, Private Corporations, vol. i, p. 608.
128 Free Ch. of Scotland v. Overton, Appeal Cases, House of Lords, 1904; Winnebrenner v. Colder, 43 Pa. St., 244.
129 Rules of Order, Scanlan, c. iii.
130 Christ's Ev. L. C., 5 Pa. Co. Court, 121.
131 In re Zion, 8 Kulp. Pa., 239.
132 In re Hebron, 9 Phil., 609.
133 U. S. v. Church, 5 Utah, 361, 394, and 538; 15 Pac., 473; 16 Pac., 723; 18 Pac., 35.
134 Neil v. Vestry, 8 Gill., 116.
135 Madison v. Baptist, 26 N. Y., 570; Stokes v. Phelps, 47 Hun., 570.
136 German, etc., 9 Pa. Co. C., 12.
137 Evenson v. Ellingson, 72 Wis., 242; 39 N. W., 330.
138 Toby v. Wareham, 54 Mass., 440.
139 Weber v. Zimmerman, 22 Md., 156; Wyncoop v. Cong., 10 La., 185.
140 Magie v. German, 13 N. J. Eq., 77.
141 Esterbrook v. Tillinghast, 71 Mass., 17.
142 South v. Clapp, 18 Barber, N. Y., 35.
143 Tilden v. Metcalf, 2 Day, Conn., 259; Heiss v. Vosburg, 59 Wis., 532; 18 N. W., 518.
144 Keller v. Tracy, 11 Ia., 530.
145 Verrian v. Methodist, 44 Abbott Pr., 424.
146 Trustees v. Hoessli, 13 Wis., 348.
147 Franke v. Mann, 106 Wis., 118; 81 N. W., 1014.
148 Den. v. Pilling, 24 N. J. L., 653.
149 Mormon v. United States, 136 U. S., 1; 33 L. Ed., 639.
150 In re Methodist, 67 Hun., 86.
151 In re Union, 6 Abb., N. C., 398.
152 First v. Brownell, 5 Hun., 464.
153 Evenson v. Ellingson, 72 Wis., 242; 39 N. W., 330.
154 Rules of Order, Scanlan, 20; Tartar v. Gibbs, 24 Md., 328; Sutter v. First, 42 Pa. St., 503.
155 Rose v. Vertin, 46 Mich., 457; 9 N. W., 491; Tuigg v. Sheehan, 101 Pa. St., 363.
156 Am. & Eng. Ency. of L., "Religious Societies."

157 Den. v. Bolton, 12 N. J. L., 206.
158 Bonacum v. Murphy, 65 Neb., 831, and 71 Neb., 463; 98 N. W., 1030; 102 N. W., 267, and 104 N. W., 180.
159 Bonacum v. Murphy, 71 Neb., 463; 104 N. W., 180; Bowden v. MacLeod, 1 Edw., N. Y., 588.
160 Congregation v. Martin, 4 Rob., La., 62.
161 Fitzgerald v. Robinson, 112 Mass., 371; Grosvenor v. United States, 118 Mass., 78; Post, 132.
162 Wardens v. Blanc, 8 Rob., La., 51.
163 Bowldin v. Alexander, 82 U. S., 131; 21 L. Ed., 69.
164 Den. v. Pilling, 24 N. J. L., 653.
165 Appeal of McAuley, 77 Pa., 397.
166 Smith v. Swormstedt, 57 U. S., 288; 14 L. Ed., 942.
167 Skilton v. Webster, Bright, Pa., 203; Mt. Helena Bp. Ch., 79 Miss., 488; 30 So. Rep., 714.
168 Smith v. Swormstedt, 57 U. S., 288; 14 L. Ed., 942.
169 Tartar v. Gibbs, 24 Md., 323; Papalion v. Manusos, 113 Ill. App., 316.
170 People v. Steele, 2 Barber, 397.
171 Stebbins v. Jennings, 10 Pickering, 172.
172 Elizabeth City v. Kennedy, Bush, 44, N. C. Law, 89.
173 Diffendorf v. Reformed Church, 20 Johns., N. Y., 12.
174 Sutton v. Trustees, 42 Pa., 503.
175 Baxter v. McDonald, 155 N. Y., 83; 49 N. E., 667.
176 Wardens v. Blanc, 8 Rob., 51.
177 Young v. Ransom, 31 Barb., 49.
178 Perry v. Wheeler, 75 Ky., 541.
179 Sheldon v. Easton, 4 Mass., 281; Congregation v. Peres, 42 Tenn., 620; Thompson v. Catholic, 22 Mass., 469.
180 Proprietors v. Proprietors, 48 Mass., 496.
181 Dempsey v. North, 98 Mich., 444; 57 N. W., 267.
182 Hackett v. Mt. Pleasant, 46 Ark., 291.
183 Chatard v. O'Donovan, 80 Ind., 20.
184 Brestor v. Burr, 120 N. Y., 427; 8 L. R. A., 710; 24 N. E., 937.
185 Walker v. Wainwright, 16 Barb., 486.
186 O'Hara v. Stack, 90 Pa., 477.
187 Stack v. O'Hara, 98 Pa. St., 213.
188 Cooper v. McKenna, 104 Mass., 284.
189 Leahy v. Williams, 141 Mass., 345.
190 State v. Winkle, 14 N. H., 480.
191 Methodist v. Sherman, 36 Wis., 404.
192 Baldwin v. McKlinch, 1 Me., 102.
193 Elizabeth City v. Kennedy, 44 N. C., 89.
194 Calkins v. Cheney, 92 Ill., 463.
195 St. Patrick's v. Daly, 116 Ill., 76; 4 N. E., 241.
196 Congregation v. Martin, 4 Rob., La., 62.
197 Meyer v. Baptist, 38 Vt., 614.
198 Congregation v. Martin, 4 Rob., 62.

199 Whittmore v. Fourth, 68 Mass., 306.
200 St. Patrick's v. Daly, 4 N. E., 241; 116 Ill., 76.
201 Tuigg v. Treacy, 104 Pa., 493.
202 Tartar v. Gibbs, 24 Md., 323.
203 Heiss v. Murphy, 40 Wis., 276, 278; Den. v. Pilling, 24 N. J. L., 653.
204 Weckerly v. Geyer, 11 Ser. R. Pa., 35.
205 Weinbrenner v. Colder, 43 Pa. St., 244.
206 People v. Tuthil, 31 N. Y., 550.
207 Price v. Lyon, 14 Conn., 280.
208 Suter v. Spangler, 4 Phil., 331.
209 Smith v. Pedigo, 145 Ind., 36; 32 L. R. A., 836; 33 N. E., 777.
210 McGuire v. Trustees, 54 Hun., 207.
211 Church v. Halverson, 42 Minn., 503; 44 N. W., 563; Day v. Bolton, 12 N. J. L., 206; Den. v. Pilling, 24 N. J. L., 653.
212 Osgood v. Bradley, 7 Me., 411.
213 Baptist v. Witherell, 24 Am. Dec., 223; 3 The Catholic Cyclopedia, 755; Contra: First R. P. Ch. v. Bowden, 10 Abb., N. C, 1. See post 134, 156.
214 Jewett v. Thames, 16 Conn., 511.
215 Chick v. Trevett, 20 Me., 462; Allen v. M. E. Church, 127 Ia., 96; 102 N. W., 808; 69 L. R. A., 255.
216 Sheehy v. Blake, 72 Wis., 411; 39 N. W., 479; 9 L. R. A., 564.
217 Chase v. Merrimac, 34 Mass., 564; Bigelow v. Congregation, 15 Vt., 370.
218 Richardson v. Butterfield, 60 Mass., 191.
219 State v. Hebrew, 31 La. Ann., 205; 33 Am. Rep., 217; Grosvenor v. United States, 118 Mass., 78; Watson v. Garbin, 54 Mo., 358.
220 State v. Getty, 69 Conn., 286; 37 At., 188.
221 Free Church of Scotland v. Overton, Appeal Cases, House of Lords, 1904; Fuchs v. Meisel, 102 Mich., 357; 32 L. R. A., 92; 60 N. W., 773.
222 Methodist v. Wood, 5 Ohio, 12.
223 McGinnis v. Watson, 41 Pa. St., 9.
224 German v. Seibert, 3 Pa. St., 282.
225 Sutter v. First, 42 Pa. St., 503.
226 Miller v. Gable, 2 Den., N. Y., 492; Eis v. Croze, 149 Mich., 62; 112 N. W., 943; Dressen v. Brameier, 56 Ia., 756; 9 N. W., 193; Amish v. Gelhaus, 71 Ia., 170; 32 N. W., 318.
227 Lamm v. Cain, 129 Ind., 486; 14 L. R. A., 518.
228 Fernald v. Lewis, 6 Me., 264.
229 Trustees v. Henschell, 48 Minn., 494; 51 N. W., 477.
230 Perry v. Tupper, 74 N. C., 722.
231 Wanner v. Emanuel, 174 Pa., 466.
232 West v. Ottesen, 80 Wis., 62; 49 N. W., 24.
233 Second v. First, 23 Conn., 255.
234 Smith v. Swormstedt, 57 U. S., 288; 14 L. Ed., 942.
235 Nelson v. Benson, 69 Ill., 27; Brown v. Porter, 10 Mass., 93.
236 Page v. Crosby, 41 Mass., 211.
237 Harper v. Straws, 53 Ky., 48; Hale v. Everett, 53 N. H., 9; Wiswell v. First, 14 Ohio St., 31; Reorganized v. Church, 60 Fed., 937; 32 L. R. A., 838; Fernstler v.

Seibert, 114 Pa., 196; 6 At., 165.
238 Shannon v. First, 42 Ky., 253.
239 Servatius v. Pichel, 34 Wis., 292; McGrath v. Finn, 16 Alb. L. J., 186; Morasse v. Borchee, 151 Mass., 567; 25 N. E., 74.
240 Farnsworth v. Storrs, 59 Mass., 412.
241 Bowldin v. Alexander, 15 Wall., 131; 21 L. Ed., 69; Ante, sec. 116, post 156.
242 In re Paulson's will, 127 Wis., 612; 107 N. W., 484.
243 Barry v. C. K. of W., 119 Wis., 362; 96 N. W., 797.
244 In re Knox, 25 Ch. Div., 542.
245 Harden v. Baptist, 51 Mich., 137; 16 N. W., 311.
246 Taylor v. Edison, 58 Mass., 522; Gray v. Christian, 137 Mass., 329.
247 Fulbright v. Higgenbotham, 133 Mo., 668; 34 S. W., 875.
248 Jones v. State, 28 Neb., 495; 44 N. W., 658; 7 L. R. A., 325.
249 Hamel v. German, 1 Weekly Note Cases, 411.
250 State v. Hebrew, 31 La. Ann., 205; 33 Am. Rep., 217.
251 Deadrick v. Lampson, 58 Tenn., 523.
252 Smith v. Pedigo, 145 Ind., 361; 32 L. R. A., 838.
253 Lucas v. Case, 9 Bush, Ky., 297.
254 Grosvenor v. U. S., 118 Mass., 78.
255 Miller v. English, 21 N. J. L., 317; 10 Cyc, 320-328; Rules of Order, Scanlan, 17.
256 State v. Crowell, 9 N. J. L., 391; Commonwealth v. Cain, 5 Ser. & R., Pa., 510.
257 Wegerle v. Geyer, 11 Ser. & R., Pa., 35.
258 Juker v. Commonwealth, 20 Pa. St., 484; St. Luke's v. Matthews, 4 Desau, S. C., 578; State v. Crowell, 9 N. J. L., 391.
259 People v. Tuthill, 31 N. Y., 550.
260 Rules of Order, Scanlan, 18, 20; 10 Cyc, 329.
261 Madison v. Baptist, 32 Howard's Pr., 335.
262 People v. Tuthill, 31 N. Y., 550.
263 Hart v. Harvey, 32 Barb., N. Y., 55.
264 Alexander v. Bowers, 79 S. W., 342.
265 Rules of Order, Scanlan, 18, 20, 23; People v. Peck, 11 Wend., N. Y., 604.
266 Rules of Order, Scanlan, 9; Gipson v. Morris, 83 S. W., Tex., 226; McCrary's Am. L. of Elections, secs. 298-300.
267 Juker v. Commonwealth, 20 Pa., 484.
268 Rules of Order, Scanlan, 23-27; Wardens v. Pope, 8 Gray, Mass., 140.
269 Den. v. Pilling, 24 N. J. L., 653.
270 Vestry v. Matthews, 4 Desau, S. C., 578.
271 Cooley's Con. Lim., 619; McCrary's Am. L. of Elections, sec. 197; Rules of Order, Scanlan, 24-27.
272 Commonwealth v. Woelper, 3 Ser. & R., Pa., 29.
273 In re Peters, 112 N. Y. Sup., 339.
274 Gram v. Prussia, 36 N. Y., 161.
275 Wall v. Johnson, 140 Ind., 445; 39 N. E., 251; Simmons v. Allison, 118 N. C., 763.
276 People v. St. Anthony, 109 N. Y., 512; 17 N. E., 408.

277 Congregation v. Martin, 4 Rob., 62; Wardens v. Blanc, 8 Rob., 51; St. Andrew's Ch. v. Schaugnessy, 63 Neb., 792; 89 N. W., 261.
278 Enos v. Church, 187 Mass., 40; 72 N. E., 253.
279 Ross v. Crockett, 14 La. Ann., 811.
280 Laight v. Noe, 12 Howard's Pr., 497; Contra: In re Williams, 105 N. Y. S., 1105; Ante, 116, 134.
281 People v. Lacoste, 37 N. Y., 192; Fadness v. Braunberg, 73 Wis., 257; 41 N. W., 84; McCrary on Am. L. of Elections, secs. 209, 264; 10 Cyc, 347; People v. Nappa, 89 Mich., 232; 50 N. W., 846.
282 Hendrickson v. Shotwell, 1 N. J. Eq., 577.
283 Congregation v. Sperry, 10 Conn., 200; 10 Cyc, 319.
284 Den. v. Pilling, 24 N. J. L., 653.
285 Smith v. Erb, 5 Gill., Md., 437.
286 People v. Peck, 11 Wend., N. Y., 604.
287 Catron v. First, 46 Ia., 106; People v. St. Anthony's, 109 N. Y., 512; 17 N. E., 408.
288 Columbia v. Gospel, 127 N. Y., 361.
289 First v. Caughey, 85 Pa., 271.
290 San Antonia v. Adams, 87 Tex., 125; 26 S. W., 1040; Hill v. Rich, 119 Mo., 9; 24 S. W., 223.
291 Hewitt v. Wheeler, 22 Conn., 577; Devos v. Gray, 22 Ohio, 159; Klopp v. Moore, 6 Kan., 27; Neil v. Spencer, 5 Ill. App., 461; United v. Vandusen, 37 Wis., 54.
292 Miller v. Church, 4 Phil., 48.
293 Brunnenmeyer v. Buhre, 32 Ill., 183.
294 N. Baptist v. Parker, 36 Barb., N. Y., 171.
295 Dennison v. Austin, 15 Wis., 334.
296 United v. Vandusen, 37 Wis., 54; MacLaury v. Hart, 121 N. Y., 636; 24 N. E., 1013.
297 Vestry v. Barksdale, 1 Strobb. Eq., S. C., 197.
298 New v. Gress, 89 Ga., 125.
299 10 Cyc, 776-9; In re Denny, 156 Ind., 104; 59 N. E., 359; 51 L. R. A., 722.
300 Rules of Order, Scanlan, 21; U. S. v. Balm, 144 U. S., 1; 12 Sup. Ct. R., 507; 36 L. Ed., 321; The Catholic Cyclopedia, vol. i, 289.
301 Cicotte v. Anciaux, 53 Mich., 227; 18 N. W., 793.
302 Trustees v. Halverson, 42 Minn., 503; 44 N. W., 663.
303 Skinner v. Richardson, 76 Wis., 464; 45 N. W., 318; Dennison v. Auston, 15 Wis., 334.
304 Vestry v. Barksdale, 1 Strobb. S. C. Eq., 197.
305 State v. Ahnapee, 99 Wis., 322; 74 N. W., 783.
306 Bowldin v. Alexander, 82 U. S., 131; 21 L. Ed., 69; The Catholic Cyclopedia, vol. iii, 755, 756.
307 Leahy v. Williams, 141 Mass., 345; 6 N. E., 78.
308 People v. Runkel, 8 Johnson, N. Y., 464.
309 Leahy v. Williams, 141 Mass., 345.
310 Rose v. Vertin, 46 Mich., 457; 9 N. W., 491; Tuigg v. Sheehan, 101 Pa., 363.
311 Freeport v. Egan, 146 Pa., 106; 23 At., 390.

312 Scott v. Thompson, 21 Ia., 599.
313 Emonds v. Termehr, 60 Ia., 92; 14 N. W., 197.
314 Wojcienchowski v. Johnknowski, 16 Pa. Sup. Ct., 444.
315 Chiniqui v. Delaire, 37 Ill., 237.
316 St. Patrick's v. Abst., 76 Ill., 252.
317 First v. Prior, 23 Hun., 271.
318 Den. v. Pilling, 24 N. J. L., 653; Rules of Order, Scanlan, 15-18.
319 German v. Pressler, 17 La. Ann., 127.
320 Appeal of McAuley, 77 Pa., 397.
321 Bethany v. Sperry, 10 Conn., 200.
322 Weber v. Zimmermann, 22 Md., 156.
323 Downs v. Bowdoin, 149 Mass., 135; 21 N. E., 294.
324 Smith v. Erb., 4 Gill., Md., 437.
325 Helbig v. Rosenberg, 86 Ia., 159; 53 N. W., 111.
326 Dahl v. Palache, 68 Cal., 248.
327 People v. Runkel, 9 Johnson, 147.
328 First v. Hillary, 51 Cal., 155.
329 Tuttle v. Cary, 7 Me., 426.
330 State v. Steward, 6 Houst., Del., 9.
331 Jones v. Cary, 6 Me., 448; Rules of Order, Scanlan, 29-30.
332 State v. Steward, 6 Houst., Del., 359.
333 Juker v. Commonwealth, 20 Pa., 484; McIlvain v. Christ's Church, 8 Phil., 507.
334 Livingston v. Trinity Church, 45 N. J. L., 230.
335 People v. Tuthill, 31 N. Y., 550.
336 Madison v. Baptist, 46 N. Y., 131.
337 Moore v. St. Thomas' Church, 4 Abb., N. Y., 51.
338 Commonwealth v. Woelper, 3 Ser. & R., 29.
339 Wardens v. Pope, 74 Mass., 140.
340 Oakes v. Hill, 6 Weekly Notes, Cas., 346.
341 Hartt v. Harvey, 32 Barb., 55.
342 Weckerly v. Geyer, 11 Ser. & R., 35.
343 People v. Church, 48 Barb., 603.
344 Allen v. Gray, 11 Conn., 95.
345 Arthur v. Norfield, 49 At., 241; 73 Conn., 718.
346 Pepin v. Societies, 23 R. I., 81; 60 L. R. A., 626.
347 Lahiff v. St. Joseph's T. A. B. S., 76 Conn., 648; 65 L. R. A., 92.
348 10 Cyc, 1067.
349 17 Cyc, 405; 2 Jones on Ev., secs. 522, 523; Conflict of L., Wharton, vol. ii, sec. 761, pp. 1496-8; Collins v. German, Am. M. I. Ass., 112 Mo. App., 209; 86 S. W., 891; Layton v. Kraft, 98 N. Y., 996.
350 Collins v. German, 112 Mo. App., 209; Sandberg v. The State, 113 Wis., 578; 89 N. W., 504.
351 Sawyer v. Baldwin, 11 Pickering, 492.
352 Finher v. Hanegen, 59 Ark., 151; 24 L. R. A., 543.
353 Mt. Zion v. Whitmore, 83 Ia., 138; 49 N. W., 846; 13 L. R. A., 198.
354 Bonacum v. Murphy, 65 Neb., 831; 98 N. W., 1030; 71 Neb., 463; 102 N. W.,

267; 104 ib., 180; Nance v. Busby, 91 Tenn., 303; 18 S. W., 874; 15 L. R. A., 801.
355 Bonacum v. Harrington, 65 Neb., 831; 91 N. W., 886.
356 Tubbs v. Lynch, 4 Harr., Del., 521.
357 Sterns v. Bedford, 21 Pickering, 114.
358 O'Donovan v. Chatard, 97 Ind., 421.
359 Baxter v. McDonald, 155 N. Y., 83; 49 N. E., 667.
360 Gibbs v. Gilead, 38 Conn., 153.
361 Stack v. O'Hara, 98 Pa., 213.
362 29 Cyc, 204, and "Religious Societies"; Am. & Eng. Cyc. of L., "Religious Societies" and "Beneficial Societies"; 2 Benefit Societies & L. Insurance, Bacon, secs. 400a and 450a.
363 Farnsworth v. Storrs, 59 Mass., 412.
364 Hatfield v. Delong, 24 Ind. App., 343; 51 L. R. A., 751; Ryan v. Cudahy, 157 Ill., 108; 41 N. E., 760; 49 L. R. A., 353.
365 Sampsell v. Esher, 26 Weekly Law Bulletin, Ohio, 156.
366 Day v. Robinson, 12 N. J. L., 206.
367 Diffendorf v. Reformed Church, 20 Johnson, N. Y., 12.
368 Chase v. Cheney, 58 Ill., 509.
369 Catholic Dictionary, Addis & Arnold, "Prescription."
370 Legal Formulary, Baart, 462.
371 Juker v. Commonwealth, 20 Pa. St., 484.
372 Beers v. Arkansas, 20 How., U. S., 527; 15 L. Ed., 991.
373 See "Benefit of the Clergy" and "Forum Ecclesiasticum," in The Catholic Cyclopedia and in the Catholic Dictionary.
374 Kuns v. Robinson, 154 Ill., 394; 40 N. E., 343; Brundage v. Deardorf, 55 Fed., 839; Watson v. Jones, 80 U. S., 679; 20 L. Ed., 666; Bird v. St. Mark's, 62 Ia., 567; 17 N. W., 747; Perry v. Wheeler, 75 Ky., 541; Powers v. Bundy, 45 Neb., 208; 63 N. W., 476; Connit v. Reformed, 54 N. Y., 551; Harrison v. Hoyle, 24 Ohio St., 254; Krecker v. Shirey, 163 Pa., 534; 30 At., 540.
375 Watson v. Jones, 80 U. S., 679; 20 L. Ed., 666.
376 Prickett v. Wells, 117 Mo., 502; 24 S. W., 52; Pounder v. Ash, 36 Neb., 564; 54 N. W., 847.
377 Atty-Gen. v. Fed., 69 Mass., 1.
378 Mt. Helen v. Jones, 79 Miss., 488; 30 So., 714.
379 Prickett v. Wells, 117 Mo., 502; 24 S. W., 52.
380 Ferraria v. Vasconcellos, 31 Ill., 25.
381 Garten v. Penick, 68 Ky., 110.
382 Brunnenmeyer v. Buhre, 31 Ill., 183.
383 Lawson v. Kolbenson, 61 Ill., 405.
384 Robertson v. Bullions, 11 N. Y., 243.
385 Papalion v. Manusos, 113 Ill. App., 316.
386 Avery v. Baker, 27 Neb., 388; 43 N. W., 174.
387 Trustees v. Trustees, 4 N. J. Eq., 77.
388 Nash v. Sutton, 117 N. C., 231; 23 S. E., 178; Wiswell v. First, 14 Ohio St., 31.
389 Mannix v. Purcell, 46 Ohio St., 102.

390 Baker v. Ducker, 79 Cal., 365; 21 Pac., 764.
391 Morris v. Dart, 67 S. C., 338; 45 S. E., 753; 100 Am. St. Rep., 734.
392 Phipps v. Jones, 20 Pa., 260.
393 Dolan v. City, 4 Gill., 394.
394 Shakers v. Watson, 68 Fed., 730.
395 61 Cen. L. J., 49 and 55; 57 C. L. J., 201.
396 Owens v. Frank, 7 Wyoming, 457; 53 Pac., 282; 47 Cen. L. J., 221.
397 Evidence, Jones, vol. iii, p. 776.
398 Gillooley v. State, 58 Ind., 182.
399 Knight v. Lee, 80 Ind., 201.
400 Colbert v. State, 125 Wis., 423; 104 N. W., 61.
401 Hills v. State, 61 Neb., 589; 85 N. W., 836.
402 Bevins v. Kline, 21 Ind., 37.
403 In re Thomas, 54 Cal., 509.
404 Rex. v. Hoy, 2 F. & F., 4.
405 Rex. v. Griffen, 6 Cox, C. C., 219.
406 Mutual v. Robinson, 19 U. S. App., 266; State v. Morgan, 196 Mo., 177; 95 S. W., 402.
407 Katzer v. City, 104 Wis., 16; 79 N. W., 745; 80 N. W., 41.
408 Vasconcellos v. Ferraria, 27 Ill., 237.
409 Foley v. Brocksmit, 119 Ia., 457; 93 N. W., 344; 97 Am. St. R., 324; 60 L. R. A., 571; 18 Cyc, 437-9.
410 Harriman v. First, 63 Ga., 186.
411 Methodist v. Sherman, 36 Wis., 404.
412 St. Patrick's v. Daly, 116 Ill., 76; 4 N. E., 241.
413 Eager v. Inhabitants, 10 Mass., 430.
414 Barnes v. Perrine, 9 Barb., N. Y., 202; Sheehy v. Blake, 77 Wis., 394; 46 N. W., 537; 69 L. R. A., 255; Cutler v. Thomas, 25 Vt., 13; Allen v. M. E. Church, 127 Ia., 96; 102 N. W., 808; 69 L. R. A., 255 Note.
415 9 Cyc, 331.
416 45 Cent. Dig., 7.
417 45 Cent. Dig., 38.
418 45 Cent. Dig., 14.
419 45 Cent. Dig., 1-54; Am. & Eng. Ency. of Law, "Subscriptions."
420 Legal Maxims, Broom, 745; Hodges v. Nalty, 104 Wis., 464; 80 N. W., 726.
421 Hodges v. Nalty, 113 Wis., 557; 89 N. W., 535; Hodges v. O'Brien, 113 Wis., 97; 88 N. W., 901.
422 Barnes v. Perine, 9 Bar., N. Y., 202.
423 Macon v. Shepard, 2 Humphrey, Tenn., 335.
424 O'Hear v. De Goesbriand, 33 Vt., 593; 80 Am. Dec., 662.
425 Bates v. Sperrell, 10 Mass., 323; Hodges v. Green, 28 Vt., 358; Pres. v. Andrus, 21 N. J. L., 225.
426 Church v. Wells, 24 Pa., 249.
427 O'Hear v. De Goesbriand, 33 Vt., 593; 80 Am. Dec., 662.
428 Proprietors v. Roswell, 66 Me., 400; Sohier v. Trinity, 109 Mass., 1; Aylward v. O'Brien, 160 Mass., 118; 35 N. E., 313; 22 L. R. A., 206.
429 Aylward v. O'Brien, 160 Mass., 118; 35 N. E., 313; 22 L. R. A., 206; O'Hear

v. De Goesbriand, 33 Vt., 593; 80 Am. Dec., 662.
430 Smith v. Bonhoff, 2 Mich., 115.
431 Vorhees v. Presbyterian, 8 Barb., 135.
432 Price v. Lyon, 14 Conn., 280.
433 Baptist v. Witherell, 3 Paige, N. Y., 296; 24 Am. Dec., 223.
434 Perrin v. Granger, 33 Vt., 101.
435 French v. Old, 106 Mass., 479.
436 Curry v. First, 2 Pittsburg, 105.
437 Succession of Gambla, 23 La. Ann., 9.
438 First v. Braydon, 91 Mass., 248.
439 Downs v. Bowdoin, 149 Mass., 135; 21 N. E., 294.
440 Trustees v. Quackenbush, 10 Johnson, 217.
441 Kellogg v. Dickenson, 18 Vt., 266.
442 Jackson v. Rounsville, 5 Metcalf, Mass., 127.
443 Murray v. Cargill, 32 Me., 517; Gay v. Baker, 17 Mass., 435; Shaw v. Beveridge, 3 Hill, N. Y., 26; Perrin v. Granger, 33 Vt., 101.
444 Vanhorn v. Tailmadge, 8 N. J. Eq., 108.
445 Fassett v. Boylston, 19 Pickering, Mass., 361.
446 Kimball v. Rowley, 24 Pickering, Mass., 347.
447 Aylward v. O'Brien, 160 Mass., 118; 35 N. E., 313; 22 L. R. A., 206; Van Houten v. Trustees, 17 N. J. Eq., 126.
448 Howard v. Stevens, 47 Vt., 262.
449 Stoddard v. Vestry, 2 Gill. & J., Md., 227.
450 City v. McIntyre, 8 Rob., La., 467.
451 Sargent v. Pierce, 43 Mass., 80.
452 Perrin v. Leverett, 13 Mass., 128.
453 Crowley v. Miller, 19 N. Y. Weekly Dig., 262.
454 Sheldon v. Vail, 28 Hun., 354.
455 Price v. Lyons, 14 Conn., 280.
456 Perrin v. Granger, 33 Vt., 101.
457 Commonwealth v. Cain, 5 Srg. & R., Pa., 510.
458 In re Bullock, 6 Dem. Sur., 335; Heiss v. Murphy, 40 Wis., 276; Ruth v. Oberbrunner, 40 Wis., 238.
459 Ruth v. Oberbrunner, 40 Wis., 238; Goesele v. Bimeler, 55 U. S., 589; 14 L. Ed., 554; Van Houten v. Trustees, 17 N. J. Eq., 126.
460 Winnepesaukee v. Gordon, 63 N. H., 505; 3 At., 426.
461 Bethel v. Carmack, 2 Md., Ch., 143; Tartar v. Gibbs, 24 Md., 323.
462 Lynch v. Pfeiffer, 110 N. Y., 33; 17 N. E., 402.
463 Enos v. Chestnut, 88 Ill., 590.
464 Walwrath v. Camel, 28 Mich., 111.
465 Harpending v. Reformed, 41 U. S., 455; 10 L. Ed., 1029.
466 Inhabitants v. Catholics, 40 Mass., 139; People v. Trinity, 22 N. Y., 44.
467 Lynch v. Pfeiffer, 110 N. Y., 33; 17 N. E., 402; Eggleston v. Doolittle, 33 Conn., 396.
468 Tomlin v. Blunt, 31 Ill. App., 234.
469 Centenary v. Parker, 43 N. J. Eq., 307; 12 At., 142.
470 Levasseur v. Martin, 11 La. Ann., 684.

471 O'Donnell v. Holden, 21 Weekly Law Bulletin, 254.
472 Walwrath v. Camel, 28 Mich., 111.
473 Fitzpatrick v. Fitzgerald, 79 Mass., 400.
474 Hubbard v. German, 34 Ia., 31.
475 In re First, 106 N. Y., 251; 12 N. E., 626; Wiswell v. First, 14 Ohio St., 31.
476 Scott v. First, 50 Mich., 528; 15 N. W., 891.
477 In re First, 106 N. Y., 251; 12 N. E., 626.
478 Katzer v. City of Milwaukee, 104 Wis., 16; 79 N. W., 745; 80 N. W., 41.
479 Beckwith v. St. Phillip's Parish, 69 Ga., 564.
480 Miller v. Chittenden, 2 Ia., 315; 4 Ia., 252; Schenectady v. Veeder, 4 Wendell, N. Y., 494.
481 St. Patrick's v. Daly, 116 Ill., 76.
482 Nobilli v. Redman, 6 Cal., 325.
483 San Antonio v. Odin, 15 Tex., 539.
484 Blair v. Odin, 3 Tex., 288.
485 Heiss v. Vosburg, 59 Wis., 532; 18 N. W., 463.
486 Santillan v. Moses, 1 Cal., 92.
487 Heiss v. Murphy, 40 Wis., 276.
488 Robertson v. Bullions, 11 N. Y., 243.
489 Hennessey v. Walsh, 55 N. H., 515.
490 Pawlet v. Clarke, 13 U. S., 292; 3 L. Ed., 735.
491 Cheever v. Pierson, 33 Mass., 266.
492 Amish v. Gelhaus, 71 Ia., 170; 32 N. W., 318.
493 Cushman v. Church, 162 Pa., 280; 29 At., 472.
494 Kulinsky v. Dambrowski, 29 Wis., 109.
495 Reed v. Church, 6 Pa. Co. Ct., 76.
496 Fulbright v. Higgenbotham, 133 Mo., 668; 34 S. W., 875; People v. Runkel, 9 Johnson, 147; Central v. Patterson, 30 N. Y. Supp., 248; Unangst v. Shortz, 5 Horton, Pa., 506.
497 Bowden v. MacLeod, 1 Edw., N. Y., 588; Gable v. Miller, 10 Paige, N. Y., 627; Wilson v. Johns, 2 Rich., S. C., Eq., 192; Ferraria v. Vasconcellos, 31 Ill., 25.
498 Antones v. Eslava's heirs, 9 Port., 527.
499 Ferraria v. Vasconcellos, 31 Ill., 25; Brunnenmeyer v. Buhre, 32 Ill., 183.
500 Organ v. Seaford, 1 Dev., N. C. Eq., 453; Post 290, 319.
501 Gram v. Prussia, 36 N. Y., 161; Reformed v. Draper, 97 Mass., 349.
502 Dochkus v. Lithuanian, 206 Pa., 25; 55 At., 779.
503 Burke v. Wall, 29 La. Ann., 38.
504 Thompson v. West, 59 Neb., 677; 82 N. W., 13; 49 L. R. A., 337.
505 Morgan v. Leslie, Wright, O., 144.
506 Consistory v. Brandow, 52 Barb., N. Y., 228.
507 Grisson v. Hill, 17 Ark., 483.
508 Scott v. Stipe, 12 Ind., 74; Mills v. Davison, 54 N. J. Eq., 659; 35 At., 1072; 35 L. R. A., 113.
509 Appeal of Tappen, 52 Conn., 412.
510 Neely v. Hoskins, 84 Me., 386; 24 At., 882.
511 Second v. Dugan, 65 Md., 460; 5 At., 415.

512 Craig v. Inhabitants, 58 Me., 479.
513 Beckwith v. St. Phillip's Church, 68 Ga., 564.
514 Mannix v. Purcell, 46 Ohio St., 102; 19 N. E., 572; 2 L. R. A., 753.
515 Draper v. Minor, 36 Mo., 290.
516 Burton's Appeal, 57 Pa. St., 213.
517 Smith v. Pedigo, 145 Ind., 361; 33 N. E., 777; 44 N. E., 363; 32 L. R. A., 838.
518 Free Ch. of Scotland v. Overton, Appeal Cases, House of Lords, 1904; McGinnis v. Watson, 41 Pa. St., 9; Ante, 278.
519 First v. Rauss, 21 Conn., 160; Watson v. Jones, 13 Wallace, 679; 20 L. Ed., 666.
520 App. v. Lutheran, 6 Pa. St., 201.
521 Keller v. Tracy, 11 Ia., 530; Happy v. Morton, 33 Ill., 398; Leftwig v. Thornton, 18 Ia., 56.
522 Watson v. Jones, 13 Wallace, 679; 20 L. Ed., 666.
523 Dolan v. Mayor, 4 Gill., Md., 394.
524 Goode v. McPherson, 51 Mo., 126.
525 Olcott v. Gabert, 86 Tex., 121; 23 S. W., 985.
526 Strong v. Doty, 32 Wis., 381.
527 Fadness v. Braunburg, 73 Wis., 257; 41 N. W., 84.
528 Weld v. May, 9 Cushing, Mass., 181.
529 Field v. Field, 9 Wendell, N. Y., 394; Stokes v. Dale, 14 N. Y., 901.
530 Hendrickson v. Shotwell, 1 N. J. Eq., 577; Calkins v. Cheney, 92 Ill., 463; Park v. Chaplain, 96 Ia., 55; 64 N. W., 674.
531 Beech v. Allen, 7 Hun., 441.
532 Catholic v. Gibbons, 3 Weekly Law Bulletin, 581.
533 Lyons v. Planters, 86 Ga., 485.
534 African v. Duru, 19 La. Ann., 302; Harrisburg v. Washburn, 29 Oregon, 150; 44 Pac., 390.
535 Lynn v. Carson, 32 Grat., Va., 170.
536 Proprietor v. Butler, 56 Mass., 597.
537 DeRuyter v. St. Peter's, 3 N. Y., 238.
538 Perrian v. Methodist, 4 Abbot's Pr., N. Y., 424; Unangst v. Shortz, 5 Horton, Pa. St., 506; Trustees v. Hoessli, 13 Wis., 348.
539 Miller v. Chittenden, 2 Ia., 315; Church v. Grace, 68 N. Y., 570; Gilmer v. Stone, 120 U. S., 586; 30 L. Ed., 734; Kinney v. Kinney's Executors, 86 Ky., 610; 6 S. W., 593.
540 St. Peter's v. German, 104 Ill., 440.
541 Kinney v. Kinney's Executors, 86 Ky., 610; 6 S. W., 593.
542 Trustees v. Manning, 72 Md., 116; 19 At., 599.
543 Morgan v. Leslie, Wright, 144.
544 U. S. v. Church, 5 Utah, 361; 15 Pac., 473.
545 In re Ticknor's estate, 13 Mich., 44; Levy v. Levy, 33 N. Y., 97.
546 Trustees v. Hilkin, 84 Md., 170; 35 At., 9.
547 Hamsher v. Hamsher, 132 Ill., 273; 23 N. E., 1123; 8 L. R. A., 556.
548 Hanson v. Little Sisters, 79 Md., 434; 32 At., 1052; Jones v. Habersham, 107 U. S., 174; 27 L. Ed., 401.
549 Church v. Grace, 68 N. Y., 570.

550 Tartar v. Gibbs, 24 Md., 323.
551 Trinitarian v. Union, 61 N. H., 384.
552 Smith v. Pedigo, 145 Ind., 361; 44 N. E., 363; 32 L. R. A., 838.
553 Miller v. English, 21 N. J. L., 317.
554 Petot v. Tucker, 21 N. Y., 267.
555 Ludlam v. Higbee, 11 N. J. Eq., 342.
556 Happy v. Morton, 33 Ill., 398.
557 Sutor v. Spangler, 4 Phil., 331.
558 Scott v. Stipe, 12 Ind., 74.
559 Commonwealth v. Dougherty, 107 Mass., 243.
560 In re Wright's estate, Myr. Prob., 213 Cal.
561 Green v. Dennis, 6 Conn., 293; Ferguson v. Hedges, 1 Harr., 524.
562 Murphy v. Dallam, 1 Bland, 529.
563 Festorazzi v. St. Joseph's, 104 Ala., 327; 18 So., 394; 25 L. R. A., 360; Ex parte Schuler, 134 Mass., 436; Seiber's Appeal, 9 At., Pa., 863; Holland v. Alcock, 108 N. Y., 312; 16 N. E., 305.
564 Festorazzi v. St. Joseph's, 104 Ala., 327; 18 So., 394; 25 L. R. A., 360.
565 McHugh v. McCole, 97 Wis., 166; 72 N. W., 352.
566 Wilson v. Perry, 29 W. Va., 169; 1 S. E., 302.
567 Jones v. Habersham, 107 U. S., 174; 27 L. Ed., 401.
568 Good v. Zook, 116 Ia., 582; 88 N. W., 376.
569 Trustees v. Sturgeon, 9 Pa. St., 321.
570 Scott v. Curle, 9 B. Mon., 17; Ante, 278, 290.
571 In re Paulson's will, 127 Wis., 612; 107 N. W., 484.
572 Robertson v. Bullions, 11 N. Y., 243.
573 62 Cen. L. J., 167.
574 Ould v. Washington, 95 U. S., 303; 24 L. Ed., 450.
575 Jones v. Habersham, 107 U. S., 174; 27 L. Ed., 401.
576 Darcy v. Kelley, 153 Mass., 433; 26 N. E., 1110.
577 Bronson v. Strouse, 57 Conn., 147; 17 At., 699.
578 Tichenor v. Brewer's, 98 Ky., 349; 33 S. W., 86.
579 Banker v. Phelan, 4 Barb., 80.
580 Bowers v. Fromm, Add., Pa., 362.
581 Germania v. Baltes, 113 Ill., 29.
582 McDonald v. Shaw, 98 S. W., 952.
583 Beaty v. Kurtz, 27 U. S., 566; 7 L. Ed., 521.
584 Heiss v. Murphy, 40 Wis., 276; Fadness v. Braunburg, 73 Wis., 257; 41 N. W., 84.
585 Coe v. Washington, 149 Mass., 543; 21 N. E., 966.
586 Clark v. Brown, 108 S. W., 421, Tex.
587 Parker v. Quinn, 23 Utah, 332; 64 Pac., 961.
588 All Saints v. Brookline, 59 N. E., 1003, Mass.
589 Green v. Outagamie, 76 Wis., 587; 45 N. W., 536.
590 Katzer v. City, 104 Wis., 16; 80 N. W., 41.
591 St. Joseph Hospital v. Ashland, 96 Wis., 636; 72 N. W., 43.
592 Ramsey v. Church, 45 Minn., 229; 47 N. W., 783.
593 Gray v. Lafayette, 65 Wis., 567; 27 N. W., 311.

594 Newport v. Masonic, 108 Ky., 333; 56 S. W., 405; 49 L. R. A., 252.
595 Trustees v. City, 122 Wis., 452; 100 N. W., 837.
596 Dahl v. Kimball, 6 Me., 171.
597 Turner v. Inhabitants, 16 Mass., 208; Goodell Mfg. Co. v. Trask, 28 Mass., 514.
598 Muzzy v. Wilkins, Smith, 1; Ebau v. Hendell, 5 Watts, 43; 30 Am. Dec., 291.
599 Miller v. Board, 19 Ill. App., 48; Municipality of Ponce v. R. C. A. Ch., 28 Sup. Ct. R., 737; Reuben Quick-Bear v. Leupp, 28 Sup. Ct. Repr., 690; Dorner v. Dist., 118 N. W., 353.
600 53 Cen. L. J., 224.
601 Hewitt v. Woman's, 73 N. H., 556; 64 At., 190.
602 Collins v. New York, 69 N. Y. Supp., 106.
603 Louisville v. Hammock, 106 S. W., Ky., 219; 14 L. R. A., N. S., 784.
604 Indianapolis v. Grant, 25 Ind., 518.
605 Newport v. Masonic, 108 Ky., 333; 56 S. W., 405; 49 L. R. A., 252.
606 McGee v. German, 13 N. J. Eq., 77.
607 Miller v. Lerch, Wall. Jr., Pa., 210.
608 St. Mary's Industrial School for Boys v. Brown, 45 Md., 310.
609 White v. Price, 108 N. Y., 661; 15 N. E., 427.
610 Sec. 5, Ky. Constitution; Contra: N. H. Constitution, art. 6.
611 Donahue v. Richards, 38 Me., 376; State v. Baily, 157 Ind., 324; 61 N. E., 730; 54 Cen. L. J., 142.
612 St. Patrick's v. Rochester, 34 How. Pr., 227.
613 People v. Board, 13 Barb., N. Y., 400.
614 Synod v. State, 2 S. Dak., 366; 50 N. W., 632; 14 L. R. A., 418.
615 State v. Hallock, 16 Nev., 373; Dorner v. School Dist., 118 N. W., Wis., 353 (Nov. 27, 1908).
616 Jenkins v. Andover, 103 Mass., 94.
617 Millard v. Board, 121 Ill., 297; 10 N. E., 669; Dorner v. School Dist., 118 N. W., Wis., 353.
618 Church v. Bullock, 100 S. W., Tex., 1025; Donahue v. Richards, 38 Me., 379; 56 C. L. J., 81.
619 State v. Board, 76 Wis., 177; 44 N. W., 967; 7 L. R. A., 330; 53 Am. R., 282; 14 L. R. A., 419; Dorner v. School Dist., 118 N. W., Wis., 353 (Nov. 27, 1908).
620 Billard v. Board, 69 Kan., 53; 76 Pac., 422; 66 L. R. A., 166.
621 Stevenson v. Hanyon, 7 Pa. Co. Ct., 585; State v. Board, 76 Wis., 177; 44 N. W., 967; 7 L. R. A., 330; State v. Scheve, 65 Neb., 853; 91 N. W., 846; 59 L. R. A., 927.
622 Dorner v. School District, 118 N. W., Wis., 353 (Nov. 27, 1908); County v. Industrial School, 125 Ill., 540; 18 N. E., 183; 1 L. R. A., 437; 8 Am. St. Rep., 386; O'Connor v. Hendrick, 184 N. Y., 421; 77 N. E., 612.
623 Board v. Minor, 23 Ohio, 250; Campanas v. Calderhead, 17 Mont., 548; 44 Pac., 83; 36 L. R. A., 277.
624 Spiller v. Woburn, 12 Allen, Mass., 127.
625 School Commissioners v. State Board, 26 Md., 505.
626 Donahue v. Richards, 38 Me., 379; 56 Cen. L. J., 81.
627 Scofield v. State, 27 Conn., 499.

628 School v. Arnold, 21 Wis., 657.
629 Sherman v. Charleston, 8 Cushing, Mass., 160; State v. Board, 116 N. W., 232; 67 Cen. L. J., 241.
630 Guernsey v. Pitkin, 32 Vt., 224.
631 Wood v. Morrow, 35 Wis., 59.
632 Anderson v. State, 3 Head, Tenn., 455.
633 Lander v. Seaver, 32 Vt., 114.
634 Stevens v. Fassett, 27 Me., 266.
635 Draper v. Cambridge, 20 Ind., 268.
636 Lane v. Baker, 12 Ohio St., 237; State v. City, 19 Ohio, 178; Van Camp v. Board, 9 Ohio St., 406.
637 Ex parte Plessy, 45 La. Ann., 80; 11 So., 948; 16 Sup. Ct. R., 1138; 163 U. S., 537; 41 L. Ed., 256; 18 L. R. A., 639.
638 State v. School Directors, 10 Ohio St., 448.
639 Jackson v. Hampden, 16 Me., 184.
640 Markwell v. Pereles, 95 Wis., 406 and 424; 69 N. W., 798 and 984.
641 Perry v. State, 113 Ga., 936; 39 S. E., 315.
642 Aycock v. Harrington, 84 Miss., 204; 36 So., 245; 65 L. R. A., 689.
643 Wright v. Bennett, 7 Ill., 587.
644 Graham v. Bennett, 2 Cal., 503.
645 State v. Harris, 63 N. C., 1.
646 Rex. v. Canon, 7 Car. and P., 438.
647 Rex. v. Griffen, 6 Cox. C. C., 402.
648 F. v. F., 1 Ch. (1902), 688.
649 In re Jacques, 82 N. Y. Sup., 986.
650 In re Marshall, 33 N. Y. S., 104.
651 Kennedy v. Borah, 226 Ill., 243; 80 N. E., 767.
652 Prieto v. Alphonso, 52 La. Ann., 631; 27 So., 153.
653 Clarkson v. Hatton, 143 Mo., 47; 44 S. W., 761; 65 Am. St. R., 635; Matter of Johnson, 98 Cal., 531; 33 Pac., 260; 21 L. R. A., 380; Schlitz v. Roenitz, 86 Wis., 31; 56 N. W., 194; 39 Am. St. R., 873; 21 L. R. A., 482; Markwell v. Pereles, 95 Wis., 406; 69 N. W., 798; 67 Cen. L. J., 197.
654 Elliott v. Elliott, 77 Wis., 634; 46 N. W., 806; 57 L. R. A., 155; 10 L. R. A., 568.
655 Cole v. State, 75 S. W., 527; 45 Tex.; Cr. App., 225; 57 Cen. L. J., 341.
656 Mutter v. Senibbs, 79 N. E., 762, Mass.
657 Commonwealth v. McAfee, 108 Mass., 458.
658 Tuttle v. Sutts, 96 Pac., 260.
659 Gleason v. Gleason, 4 Wis., 64; 14 Cyc, 846.
660 32 St. At. L., 636 and 645.
661 Chap. 1402, U. S. Laws of 1904.
662 Quick-Bear v. Leupp, 28 Sup. Ct. Rep., 690 (1908).
663 Sec. 2045, U. S. Statutes.
664 Secs. 2071 and 2072, U. S. Statutes, and Chap. 188, Laws of 1895.
665 26 St. At. L., 1014.
666 Quick-Bear v. Leupp, 28 Sup. Ct. Repr., 690; 27 St. L., 628 and 635.
667 In re Lehah-puc-ka-chee, 98 Fed., 429.

668 Chap. 503, Laws of 1888.
669 Chap. 3, Laws of 1897.
670 61 Cen. L. J., 101, 289; 62 Cen. L. J., 215, 219.
671 McCann v. County, 6 Mont., 297.
672 Hubbard v. Railway, 104 Wis., 160; 80 N. W., 454.
673 Hochheimer on Custody of Infants, sec. 54; People v. Turner, 55 Ill., 280; People v. Park, 41 N. Y., 21, 33.
674 Kleizer v. Symes, 40 Ind., 562; Etchison v. Pergeson, 88 Ga., 620; 15 S. E., 680; Lucas v. Case, 72 (9 Bush) Ky., 297; York v. Pease, 68 Mass., 288; Piper v. Woolman, 43 Neb., 280; 61 N. W., 588; O'Donahue v. McGovern, 23 Wendell, N. Y., 26; Servatius v. Pichel, 34 Wis., 292.
675 Combes v. Rose, 8 Blackf., 155; Servatius v. Pichel, 34 Wis., 292; Etchison v. Pergeson, 88 Ga., 620; 15 S. E., 680.
676 Gardener v. Anderson, Fed. Case, 5220; Rector v. Smith, 11 Ia., 302.
677 See "Excommunication," ante. Servatius v. Pichel, 34 Wis., 292; 11 L. R. A., 592.
678 Shelton v. Nause, 46 Ky., 128.
679 Fawcett v. Charles, 13 Wendell, 473.
680 54 Cen. L. J., 313.
681 Hellstern v. Katzer, 103 Wis., 391; 79 N. W., 429.
682 Hills v. State, 61 Neb., 589; 85 N. W., 836.
683 Konkle v. Haven, 140 Mich., 472; 103 N. W., 850.
684 Klos v. Zahorik, 113 Ia., 161; 84 N. W., 1046.
685 Libel and Slander, Townsend, secs. 233, 234; 25 Cyc, 390, 398, 411.
686 Grace v. Dempsey, 75 Wis., 313; 43 N. W., 1127; Grace v. McArthur, 76 Wis., 641; 45 N. W., 518.
687 25 Cyc, 390, 398.
688 62 Cen. L. J., 180.
689 Libel and Slander, Townsend, p. 182 (notes).
690 Libel and Slander, Townsend, sec. 177; 25 Cyc, 398; Edwards v. Bell, 8 Moore, 467.
691 Remington v. Congdon, 2 Pickering, 315; Bradley v. Heath, 12 Pickering, 163.
692 McConckle v. Binns, 5 Binns, Pa., 340.
693 MacBride v. Allis, 9 Rich., S. C., 313.
694 State v. Riggs, 22 Vt., 322.
695 Commonwealth v. Batchelder, Thach., Mass., Cr. Cas., 191.
696 Shoe & L. v. Thompson, 18 Abbot's Pr., N. Y., 413.
697 Sans v. Joerris, 14 Wis., 663.
698 5 Cyc, 715; "Disorderly Conduct," 14 Cyc, 467.
699 14 Cyc, 540.
700 Williams v. State, 83 Ala., 78; 3 So., 616.
701 Hull v. State, 120 Ind., 153; 22 N. E., 117.
702 Hunt v. State, 3 Tex., 116.
703 State v. Kirby, 108 N. C., 772; 12 S. E., 1045.
704 Commonwealth v. Sigman, 2 Clark, Pa., 36.
705 State v. Wright, 41 Ark., 410; Tanner v. State, 126 Ga., 77; 54 S. E., 914.

706 State v. Shepherd, 54 S. C., 178; 32 S. E., 146; 14 Cyc, 467, 540.
707 Martin v. State, 65 Tenn., 234.
708 State v. Leighton, 35 Me., 195.
709 Marvin v. State, 19 Ind., 181.
710 Brown v. State, 46 Ala., 175.
711 State v. Turkhaw, 69 N. C., 215.
712 Richardson v. State, 5 Tex. App., 470.
713 U. S. v. Brooks, 4 Cranch, C. C., 427.
714 People v. Crowley, 23 Hun., 412; McLane v. Mallock, 7 Ind., 525.
715 Kinney v. State, 38 Ala., 224; State v. Lusk, 68 Ind., 264; State v. Edwards, 32 Mo., 548; Tanner v. State, 126 Ga., 77; 54 S. E., 914.
716 MacLean v. Mallock, 7 Ind., 525.
717 Wall v. Lee, 34 N. Y., 141.
718 Meyer v. Baker, 120 Ill., 567; 12 N. E., 79; Commonwealth v. Bearse, 132 Mass., 542; 42 Am. R., 450; West v. State, 28 Tenn., 66; Cramer v. Marks, 64 Pa. St., 151.
719 5 Cyc, 713; Commonwealth v. Linn, 158 Pa., 22; 27 At., 843; 22 L. R. A., 353.
720 Gaines v. State, 75 Tenn., 410; Holcombe v. Cornish, 8 Conn., 375; Bodenheimer v. State, 60 Ark., 10; 28 S. W., 507.
721 State v. Chandler, 2 Har., Del., 553.
722 Commonwealth v. Kneeland, 37 Mass. (20 Pick), 206.
723 People v. Ruggles, 8 Johnson, 225.
724 State v. Chandler, 2 Harr., Del., 553.
725 State v. Pepper, 68 N. C., 259.
726 Odell v. Garnett, 4 Blackf., Ind., 549.
727 People v. Porter, 2 Park, N. Y. Cr., 14.
728 State v. Chandler, 2 Harr., Del., 553; Commonwealth v. Kneeland, Thach., Mass. Cr. Cas., 346.
729 Miller v. State, 76 Ind., 310.
730 Petty v. State, 58 Ark., 1; 22 S. W., 654.
731 Splane v. Commonwealth, 12 At., Pa., 431.
732 Commonwealth v. Keiten, 1 Monag., 368.
733 Cain v. Daly, 74 S. C, 480; 55 S. E., 110.
734 Ex parte Jentisch, 112 Cal., 468; 44 Pac., 803.
735 State v. Lorey, 66 Tenn., 95.
736 State v. Krech, 10 Wash., 166; 38 Pac., 1001.
737 People v. Havenor, 149 N. Y., 195; 43 N. E., 541; 3 L. R. A., 689; State v. Dolan, 13 Idaho, 693; 92 Pac., 995; 14 L. R. A., N. S., 1259.
738 Flag v. Inhabitants, 58 Mass., 243; Doyle v. Lynn, 118 Mass., 195.
739 Hayden v. Mitchell, 103 Ga., 431; 30 S. E., 287.
740 Roth v. Hacks, 68 Mo. App., 283.
741 Hofer v. Cowan, 55 Cen. L. J., 290.
742 Byrant v. Watson, 127 Ind., 42; 26 N. E., 687; Allen v. Duffy, 43 Mich., 1; 4 N. W., 427; 11 L. R. A., 63; Dale v. Knapp, 98 Pa., 389.
743 Society v. Commonwealth, 52 Pa., 125; Parker v. State, 84 Tenn., 476.
744 McCabe v. Father Matthews, 24 Hun., 149; People v. Young, 67 Barb., 357.

745 Philadelphia v. Lehman, 56 Md., 209; Kroer v. People, 78 Ill., 294.
746 Fox v. Abel, 2 Conn., 541.
747 Bryant v. Inhabitants, 30 Me., 193; Tracy v. Jenks, 32 Mass., 465.
748 Carpenter v. Crane, 1 Root, Conn., 98.
749 Judefinde v. State, 78 Md., 510; 28 At., 405; 22 L. R. A., 721, note.
750 55 Cen. L. J., 44; 56 Cen. L. J., 261; State v. Cheneworth, 163 Ind., 94; 71 N. E., 197; 59 Cen. L. J., 202.
751 Speed v. Tomlinson, 73 N. H., 46; 59 At., 376; 68 L. R. A., 432.
752 State v. Rodgers, 128 N. C., 576; 38 S. E., 34.
753 U. S. v. Moore, 104 Fed., 78.
754 Constant v. Rector, 4 Daly, 1.
755 Frederickson v. W. R. Cem. Ass., 133 Wis., 502; 113 N. W., 1023.
756 14 Op. Atty-Gen., 27; secs. 4780-4782, U. S. Statutes; 16 Op. Atty-Gen., 13.
757 20 St. at L., 281.
758 Sohier v. Trinity Ch., 109 Mass., 1; City v. Town, 82 Wis., 374; 52 N. W., 425.
759 Trustees v. Manning, 72 Md., 116; 19 At., 599.
760 Porch v. St. Bridget's, 81 Wis., 599; 51 N. W., 1007.
761 In re Highland, 4 Pa. Dist. Rep., 653.
762 Commonwealth v. Fisher, 7 Phil., 264; Bourland v. Springdale, 158 Ill., 458; 42 N. E., 86.
763 City v. Watson, 56 N. J. L., 667; 24 L. R. A., 843; 49 Cen. L. J., 307.
764 Coates v. City, 7 Cowan, N. Y., 585; Humphrey v. Frost, 109 N. C., 132; 13 S. E., 793; City v. Austin, 87 Tex., 330; 28 S. W., 528; 47 Am. St. R., 114.
765 Stockton v. City, 42 N. J. Eq., 531; 9 At., 203; First v. Meyers, 5 Okla., 819; 50 Pac., 70; 38 L. R. A., 329.
766 Steams v. Manchester, 63 N. H., 390; Henry v. Trustees, 48 Ohio, 671; 30 N. E., 1122.
767 Upjohn v. Board, 46 Mich., 542; 9 N. W., 845.
768 Edwards v. Stonington, 20 Conn., 466.
769 Oakland v. People, 93 Tex., 569; 57 S. W., 27; 55 L. R. A., 503.
770 Louisville v. Nevin, 73 Ky., 549; First v. Hazel, 63 Neb., 844; 89 N. W., 378.
771 Page v. Simons, 63 N. H., 17.
772 Wygant v. McLaughlin, 39 Or., 429; 64 Pac., 867; 54 L. R. A., 636; 53 Cen. L. J., 48.
773 Trustees v. Manning, 72 Md., 116; 19 At., 599; Close v. Glenwood, 107 U. S., 466; 2 Sup. Ct. R., 267; 27 L. Ed., 408; Matter of Bd. of Street Opening, 133 N. Y., 329; 31 N. E., 102; 28 Am. St. R., 640; 16 L. R. A., 180.
774 In re Waldron, 26 R. I., 84; 58 At., 453; 67 L. R. A., 118; Wright v. Hollywood, 112 Ga., 884; 38 S. E., 94; 52 L. R. A., 621.
775 Perkins v. Mass., 138 Mass., 361.
776 Wright v. Hollywood, 112 Ga., 884; 38 S. E., 94.
777 People v. Trustees, 21 Hun., 184; McGuire v. St. Pat. C. C., 3 N. Y. Sup., 781; Baltimore v. Manning, 72 Md., 116; 19 At., 599.
778 Palmer v. Cypress, 122 N. Y., 429; 25 N. E., 983.
779 Conger v. Weyant, 55 Hun., 605.
780 Baltimore v. Manning, 72 Md., 116; 19 At., 599.

843 Am. & Eng. Ency. of L., "Stara decisis," "Res judicata"; 67 Central L. Journal, 255; Pautz v. Plankinton, 126 Wis., 37; 105 N. W., 482; Whittaker v. Mich. M. L. Ins. Co., 83 N. E., 899.
844 Bonacum v. Murphy, 71 Neb., 463; 104 N. W., 180.
845 U. S. Bankruptcy Act, sec. 1, sub-sec. 25.
846 20 Cyc, 457.
847 20 Cyc, 1243; Insolvent Corporations, Wait, sec. 637.
848 20 Cyc, 469.
**